THE
SHELLFISH
COOKBOOK

THE

SHELLFISH

COOKBOOK

the definitive shellfish cookbook with more than 200 new and traditional recipes

by

ARTHUR and NANCY HAWKINS

HASTINGS HOUSE · PUBLISHERS
New York, N.Y. 10022

Library of Congress Cataloging in Publication Data

Hawkins, Arthur.
    The shellfish cookbook.

    Includes index.
    1. Cookery (Shellfish) I. Hawkins, Nancy. II. Title.
TX753.H26 1981   641.6'94   81-7050
ISBN 0-8038-6778-6   AACR2

Published simultaneously in Canada by
Saunders of Toronto, Ltd., Don Mills, Ontario

Printed in the United States of America

CONTENTS

INTRODUCTION

Crustaceans, mollusks, gastropods, cephalopods
and all those delicious creatures of the sea

All those delectable—sometimes strange-looking—creatures that inhabit the shallow-water shores and deepwater shores of the world are different: different in size, shape and conformation, and in action—different in the ways they live and eat and love—and different in taste. They are also related, sometimes in many ways.

They all have shells which, however, vary greatly from the sometimes fragile segmented ones of the crab, crayfish and lobster to the heavy armor of the clam, oyster, conch and abalone. There are shellfishes possessing two protective shells hinged together (bivalves), and those with only one, such as the abalone. And finally there are shellfishes that seem not to have any shell at all (the octopuses, squids and cuttlefishes). But even these, on closer inspection, will be seen to own at least a rudimentary shell, all that is left after the process of its evolution. The octopus's shell has become its "beak." The cuttlefish's shell, worn internally, has become a small, flat pecking treat for caged canaries.

Shellfishes have other properties in common. Regardless of how greatly they may vary in appearance, they all have mouths, digestive, excretory and reproductive systems. And they all have gills.

Far more interesting than the similarities in shellfishes are their differences. There are shellfishes that swim and those that crawl along the ocean floor seeking food. There are those that just sit there and wait for food to come to them. And there are shellfishes that do not go near the water—land crabs, escargots. There are giant crabs, clams and squids that stir the imagination of storytell-

7

ers. There are tiny crabs which live as guests in oyster shells . . . and oysters, themselves, not much larger than a thumbnail.

There are wonderful differences in the texture, consistency and flavor of the various shellfishes. It is all of these differences that make these creatures so attractive to epicures and gourmets all over the world.

To help you get a clearer understanding of the relationship—the similarities and differences—of all these delicious little animals, which we are recommending that you cook and serve for dinner, we offer herewith this quick genealogical guide:

THE SHELLFISH FAMILY TREE FOR LAYMEN

Shellfish

Mollusks		*Crustaceans*
Univalves	*Bivalves*	Crabs
(*Gastropods*)	Clams	Crayfishes
	Mussels	American Lobsters
Abalones	Oysters	Spiny Lobsters
Conchs	Scallops	Shrimps
Periwinkles		
Sea Urchins		
Snails		
Whelks		
(*Cephalopods*)		
Cuttlefishes		
Octopuses		
Squids		

And now for your further assistance, a few useful definitions, just so you will know what we are talking about:

SHELL-FISH: An aquatic animal (not a fish in the ordinary sense), having a shell.

MOL-LUSK: An invertebrate characterized by a calcareous shell of one or two pieces that wholly or partially encloses a soft unsegmented body; and provided with mantle, gills, mouth, digestive, reproductive and excretory organs.

CRUS-TA-CEAN: A class of shellfish having a segmented, hard-crusted body joined together by flexible membranes, and provided with mantle, gills, mouth, digestive, reproductive and excretory organs. Decapod crustaceans (crabs, lobsters, crayfishes, shrimps) have a pair of antennae and ten legs, two of which, in the case of swimmers, have flattened ends serving as paddles, and two of which have evolved as claws varying in size from very large to almost nonexistent.

OC-TO-POD: A cephalopod having eight arms.

DEC-A-POD: A crustacean having ten legs. Or a cephalopod with ten arms.

O-PER-CU-LUM: A disc-shaped trapdoor of a fish-scalelike material covering the opening of gastropods.

GAS-TRO-POD: A class of mollusk having one shell or valve, usually spirally curved, and provided with all the organs of a mollusk plus a muscular foot for locomotion.

CEPH-A-LO-POD: The most highly organized class of mollusk, provided with all the organs of a mollusk plus tentacles attached to the head. Cephalopods have outgrown their shells which have become atrophied.

ECH-I-NOI-DE-A: A class of echinoderms of rounded form covered with projecting spines, including the sea urchins.

UN-I-VALVE: Having one valve or shell.

BI-VALVE: Having two valves or shells united by a hinge and manipulated by one or more adductor muscles.

Marketing Forms for Shellfishes

Although great progress has been made in recent years in preserving, packaging and merchandising, shellfishes are by no means available in all parts of the country. But even in cities removed from Atlantic, Pacific and Gulf fishing grounds, some shellfishes in some form of treatment—mostly freezing or canning—are regularly and readily on hand. Along coastal areas the choice is wide and generally plentiful. The following chart will give you a quick assessment of the merchandizing forms to be expected.

	Live	Uncooked, in Shell	Uncooked, Shelled	Cooked, in Shell	Cooked, Shelled	Frozen, in Shell	Frozen, Shelled	Canned	Smoked
CRUSTACEANS									
Crabs	•	•		•	•	•	•	•	•
Crayfishes	•			•		•		•	
Lobsters, Amer.	•			•		•	•	•	•
Lobsters, Spiny				•		•	•	•	
Shrimps		•	•	•	•	•	•	•	•
BIVALVE MOLLUSKS									
Clams	•	•	•					•	•
Mussels	•	•	•				•	•	•
Oysters	•	•	•				•	•	•
Scallops			•				•		•
UNIVALVE MOLLUSKS									
Abalones			•		•		•	•	•
Conchs & Whelks	•	•	•				•	•	
Periwinkles	•								
Snails	•	•			•			•	•
Sea Urchins	•								
Octopuses		•	•			•	•	•	•
Squids		•	•			•	•	•	•

Part One

CRUSTACEANS

CRABS
CRAYFISHES
AMERICAN LOBSTERS
SPINY LOBSTERS
SHRIMPS

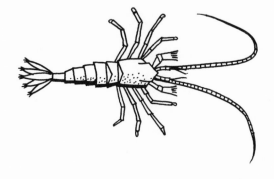

CRABS

Crabs, like lobsters, crayfishes and shrimps, are crustaceans, identified by thin segmented shells and 10 legs.

Crabs may be the most interesting, most numerous and most versatile of all the shellfishes. There are crabs that swim and those that crawl along the sea bottom and across the land. Crabs are both the largest and the smallest of all crustaceans.

The enormous Alaska King Crab, a leggy creature with tiny claws, has a body measuring only 5 to 6 inches across. It can't even swim. But it grows to an average of 8 to 10 pounds and measures 3 feet or more from tip to tip. The King inhabits only the coldest waters of Alaska and the Aleutian Islands. The supply is fast dwindling and the United States government has imposed regulations on the size and quantity that may be taken commercially. The Snow Crab, similar but somewhat smaller, is rapidly taking the place of its larger cousin in many markets.

The tiny Oyster Crab, when still in the larva stage, moves into the shell of an oyster and spends its life there, neither swimming nor moving about but sharing the food pumped in by its host. Pale pink in color and with a soft shell that never grows hard, this little creature seldom grows larger than a little fingernail, but it has a delicately delicious flavor and is highly prized for use in fish sauces.

A very important crab gastronomically is the Dungeness (pronounced with a soft g). Found along the Pacific Coast from the Aleutian Archipelago to Baja California, it has a large reddish-

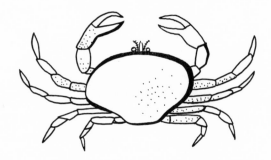

brown body measuring up to 10 to 12 inches across. It yields a plentiful supply of sweet, tender meat, very popular in the restaurants along the Embarcadero in San Francisco.

There is the Stone Crab, which lives in the sands of the Florida Keys and environs. This little crab has a body measuring only 3 to 4 inches across, but it grows disproportionately large claws gaudily tinted cream and red and tipped with black. The claws alone are taken, usually steamed, cracked and dipped into butter or a piquant sauce. The crab itself is usually returned to its habitat to grow new claws.

Then there is the little 3-inch Green Crab; the Calico Crab (or Sand Crab or Lady Crab); the 4-inch Jonah (also called Rock Crab), a smaller cousin of the Dungeness; the Pacific spidery Spider Crab (or Snow or Queen or Tanner); and the deepwater Red Crab weighing up to 2½ pounds.

If these aren't enough, add to the list the White or Mulatto Crab that lives on land in Western Florida, Bermuda, Cuba, the Bahamas and other West Indian islands. This ubiquitous little land crab scampers in and out of holes dug into the soft earth in tropical and near-tropical areas. Measuring up to 4 to 5 inches across its rounded body, it possesses stout little legs and substantial claws. Its quickness makes the land crab difficult to catch, but a suitable trap placed over the entrance hole in the ground will bring sufficient results to satisfy the modest demand.

Most shellfish fanciers agree that none of these crabs can equal in number, flavor or commercial value the great Blue Crab found in the bays and inlets of the Atlantic Coast from Cape Cod to Florida to the Gulf of Mexico. Chesapeake Bay, the most generous provider of Blue Crabs, measures a mere 200 miles from the Susquehanna to the Virginia Capes, but, with a rugged shallow shoreline and innumerable river inlets, it strings out to nearly 4,000 miles, a fertile home for lots of Blue Crabs.

The scrappy, delicious Blue measures up to 6 inches across, is dark green on top and creamy white beneath, and has 2 large meaty blue-tipped claws. It is caught with drop lines, trot lines and nets, and is dredged. As the crab grows, it periodically sloughs its shell, which no longer fits it. For a brief period it thus becomes the softshell crab so much sought after by gourmets; it also becomes the helpless prey of other denizens of the bay. The crab industry, however, does not depend upon lucky timing to catch softshells, but captures hardshells or "peelers" just as they are about to slough and stores them in bins to await the critical moment when they are promptly removed from the water before calcification of the new shells sets in.

How to Buy

According to the United States Department of Interior, crabs are our second most popular shellfish, second only to shrimps, thanks largely to modern processes and marketing methods which make them available almost anywhere in the country.

Close to their home grounds crabs may be bought live, but in more distant areas they are marketed cooked in the shell or frozen. Blue crabs are graded according to size as "mediums," "larges," "jumbos" and "jimmies." Cooked hardshell crabs must be kept refrigerated, iced or frozen until used. Softshell Dungeness crabs are not allowed to be marketed by California law, but the mature Dungeness, steamed and frozen, is found throughout the country. Usually weighing from ¾ to 1½ pounds, 1 large Dungeness will serve 2 delighted eaters. The claws and legs of King and Snow crabs are steamed, frozen and marketed all over the country. The claws of Stone crabs can be found in some Eastern specialty stores during the fall and winter.

Crab meat from all varieties can be found canned, but that most in demand is Blue Claw, steamed and pasteurized and packed in 1-pound cans in several grades: lump or backfin (for use in recipes where appearance is important, as in cocktails and salads), flake meat (small pieces of meat from the rest of the body), regular and claw meat.

When buying live crabs, be sure they move when picked up. When buying any crab or crab meat, be sure it smells sweet.

How to Prepare

To clean hardshell crabs:

a. Drop live crabs into large pot containing 2 cups of boiling water and ½ cup vinegar, seasoned with 1 teaspoon cayenne pepper. Cover and steam for 10 minutes, or until shells turn pink. Remove and cool.
b. Break off claws and legs at body. Crack and remove meat.
c. Pull off top shell from body.
d. Scrape away whitish gills from sides.
e. Remove and discard spongy digestive organs located in middle of body.
f. Break body in two along central crease.
g. Slice off top of inner skeleton beginning at front.

Remove meat from back fin and other pockets.

To clean softshell crabs (frozen crabs have already been cleaned):

    a. With a sharp knife cut off face and eyes.
    b. Lift up shell at each point and clean out.
    c. Wash in cold running water.

To clean land crabs:

Clean like any hardshell crab, but first purge for 5 to 6 days in a crate or box containing cornmeal and a saucer of water to remove impurities.

How to Store

Live crabs of all varieties, both softshell and hardshell, will keep on a bed of cracked ice for up to a week. Softshells should be placed on their backs so that they may better retain their juices. Steamed crabs will safely last in the refrigerator for an equal length of time. All crabs may be kept frozen for as long as a month but, once thawed, should not be refrozen. Crab meat, usually found steamed and packed in vacuum tins, can be kept in the refrigerator or on ice for several days, but once opened should be put to use without delay, even if pasteurized.

CHESAPEAKE BAY CRAB FEAST

On almost any summer weekend in the Chesapeake Bay region of Maryland, Delaware or Virginia, if you look carefully, you are likely to find a crab feast in session. If you can succeed in getting yourself included, you'll never forget the experience.

Great washtubs of hard crabs are steamed and consumed, usually at picnic-type tables covered with newspapers. The utensils employed are wooden clubs or mallets (for cracking claws) and sharply pointed knives. Since the sweet crab meat that is extracted from the shell is most often laced with cayenne and other nice spices, a plentiful supply of cold beer is essential.

If you are a crab fancier, you will find it hard to stop eating—and before you have finished, you might discover that you have put away 6 to 8 crabs, or even more.

The crab feast has been going on for a long time. Marylanders claim that it is as old as the New England clambake.

If you would like to cook up a modest little feast of your own, in kitchen or backyard, here's how you go about it:

Take a large pot or kettle and arrange somehow to fit a grill into it a few inches from the bottom. Pour in 1 cup vinegar, 2 cups water, 1 tablespoon black pepper, 1 tablespoon dry mustard, 1 teaspoon cayenne, and 1 teaspoon curry powder, mace, or coriander, or use crab boil (see Index).

Turn the heat up; when the steam begins to rise, toss in 2 dozen crabs, one at a time so that you can be sure they are all alive, and clamp the lid on tightly. The crabs will cook in about 10 minutes; they are done when they are pink. The grill will keep them from becoming waterlogged in their own juices.

HOT CRAB CLAWS

½ pound butter
½ garlic clove, minced
dash of Tabasco
½ teaspoon salt

1 can (10 ounces) crab claws
   from blue crabs
paprika

Melt the butter in a heavy skillet; add the garlic, Tabasco and salt.

Gently sauté the claws for about ½ minute on each side. Dust with paprika and serve with cocktails.

4 servings

CRACKED STONE CRAB CLAWS

Crack the claws of thawed frozen stone crab claws, or fresh claws steamed, and dip into drawn butter, mayonnaise or the sauce of your choice (see Index).

HOT CRAB-MEAT CANAPÉS

2 tablespoons butter
juice of ½ lemon
1 pound fresh lump or back
    fin crab meat from blue
    crabs
1 ounce Cognac

salt
cayenne
buttered toast points
paprika

Melt the butter in a heavy skillet; add the lemon juice and crab meat and sauté for a few minutes. Stir carefully; do not break up the crab lumps.

Pour in the Cognac, season to taste, and serve on toast points garnished with paprika.

6 servings

This recipe may be used also for lobster meat.

FRIED CRAB FINGERS

Crack Dungeness legs, dip them into beaten egg and then into cracker crumbs, and panfry them in butter until brown. Or fry them in deep fat.

Serve with melted butter.

CRACKED CRAB LOUIS

Nobody seems to know the exact recipe for the original Louis Sauce, which was invented in Portland, Oregon. James Beard, who also comes from Oregon, says that it consisted of mayonnaise (1 cup), whipped cream (⅓ cup), chili sauce (⅓ cup), 1 tablespoon grated onion and a pinch of cayenne.

A Dungeness crab will serve two. Cut it into halves, crack the legs and back section, and serve chilled with Louis Sauce or your favorite.

SHE CRAB SOUP

It is difficult to visit a Charleston, S.C., restaurant without discovering She Crab Soup on the menu—although it is equally difficult to find this delicacy in any other part of the country. Why "she" crabs? Because they are the crabs with roe. If you cannot find female crabs in the market, crumbled yolk of hard-cooked egg will serve as a fair substitute.

1 tablespoon butter
1 tablespoon flour
1 quart milk
2 cups crab meat with the
    eggs
1 tablespoon minced onion
½ teaspoon Worcestershire
    sauce

pinch of grated mace
salt and pepper
4 tablespoons dry sherry wine
½ cup heavy cream, whipped
paprika
minced celery

Melt the butter in the top section of a double boiler over steaming water; blend in the flour until smooth and gradually pour in the milk, stirring constantly.

Add the crab meat and eggs, onion, Worcestershire, mace, and salt and pepper to taste. Stir well and cook for about 20 minutes.

Put 1 tablespoon of sherry in the bottom of each of 4 bowls, fill with soup, and top with whipped cream. Sprinkle with paprika and celery.

6 servings

DELAWARE CRAB SOUP

2 tablespoons butter
1 tablespoon flour
2 cups water
½ pound crab meat, fresh or
    canned
1 onion, chopped
1 celery rib, chopped

1 parsley sprig, chopped
pinch of thyme
dash of Tabasco
½ teaspoon salt
pinch of pepper
3 cups hot milk

Melt the butter; add the flour and brown it. Stir in the water. Add the crab meat, vegetables and seasonings. Cover and simmer for 30 minutes.

Pour in the hot milk, and stir. Check seasonings and add more if needed.

4 servings

MARYLAND CRAB SOUP, SHORE STYLE

4 tablespoons butter
1 onion, chopped
1 green pepper, chopped
2 quarts Fish Stock (see
    Index) or clam broth
½ cup uncooked rice
3 tomatoes, peeled and diced
1 teaspoon Worcestershire
    sauce

meat of 2 large steamed crabs
1 pound fresh okra, cut into
    1-inch pieces; or 1
    package (10 ounces)
    frozen okra; or 1 pound
    canned sliced okra
salt and pepper
chopped parsley

Melt the butter in a large pot; sauté the onion and green pepper in the butter for 10 minutes.

Add the fish stock and rice; simmer for 15 minutes.

Add the tomatoes, Worcestershire, crab meat and okra; simmer for 20 minutes longer.

Season to taste and serve, sprinkled with chopped parsley.

6 to 8 servings

LOUISIANA CRAB SOUP

1 teaspoon butter
2 tablespoons lard
1 large onion, chopped
1 garlic clove, chopped
6 ripe tomatoes, peeled,
    chopped, and with seeds
    removed

½ teaspoon dried thyme
1 tablespoon chopped parsley
½ teaspoon dried marjoram
salt and pepper
1 quart, or more, hot water
1 pound crab meat, fresh or
    canned
juice of 2 lemons

Melt butter and lard in a large kettle; sauté the onion and garlic in the fat for 5 minutes, or until brown.

Add the chopped tomatoes, cover, and simmer for a few minutes longer.

Add the herbs, seasonings to taste and hot water. Cover and simmer for about 30 minutes. Add the crab meat and cook for 15 minutes longer.

Adjust seasoning, add the lemon juice, and serve.

4 to 6 servings

This recipe may be used also for crayfish meat.

CRAB BISQUE À LA RECTOR

3 tablespoons butter
3 tablespoons flour
1 quart milk
½ teaspoon salt
pinch of pepper
pinch of grated nutmeg
1 tablespoon Worcestershire
    sauce

½ pound crab meat, fresh or
    canned
3 tablespoons sherry wine
½ cup unsweetened whipped
    cream
paprika

Melt the butter, blend in the flour, and stir in the milk gradually. Cook over low heat until sauce is thickened and smooth.

Add the seasonings and simmer for 2 minutes.

Stir in the crab meat. Heat.

Stir in the sherry. Serve in cups, topped with whipped cream and a dusting of paprika.

4 to 6 servings

CREAM OF CRAB SOUP

2 hard-cooked eggs
½ pound crab meat, fresh or
    frozen
2 tablespoons butter, melted

1 tablespoon flour
1 quart milk
½ cup cream

Remove the yolks from the hard-cooked eggs and rub them through a sieve; chop the whites.

Put the crab meat, egg yolks and whites and the butter in the top section of a double boiler over steaming water. Stir in the flour, then the milk. Blend well. Heat for 15 minutes.

Remove from heat and cool. Stir in the cream. Heat again and serve hot.

4 servings

This recipe may be used also for crayfish meat.

CRAB JAMBALAYA

½ cup chopped bacon
½ cup chopped onion
½ cup chopped celery
½ cup chopped green pepper
1 can (16 ounces) tomatoes
¼ cup uncooked rice

1 tablespoon Worcestershire
    sauce
½ teaspoon salt
few grains of cayenne
1 pound fresh crab meat (any
    kind)

Fry the bacon in a heavy skillet until lightly browned. Add the onion, celery and green pepper; cook until vegetables are tender.

Add the tomatoes, rice and seasonings; cover and simmer for 20 minutes, or until rice is tender.

Add the crab meat, heat, and serve.

6 servings

This recipe may be used also for shrimps.

SAN FRANCISCO CRAB CIOPPINO

3 live Dungeness crabs
1 cup chopped onion
1 cup chopped parsley
1 cup olive oil
2 cans (16 ounces each)
  tomatoes

2 tablespoons tomato paste
2 teaspoons chopped fresh
  basil, or 1 teaspoon dried
salt and pepper

Kill the crabs by cutting off the faces with a sharp knife. Remove and discard the shells, the whitish-colored gills and the spongy digestive organs located in the middle of the body. Slice off the top of the inner skeleton and crack the claws.

Place crabs in a large kettle, and add the onion, parsley and olive oil. Cover and simmer for 15 minutes.

Add tomatoes, tomato paste and basil, cover, and cook for 30 minutes. Add seasoning to taste.

Serve with chunks of Italian or French bread.

6 servings

BALTIMORE CRAB IMPERIAL

The Old Hotel Rennert in Baltimore was a consistent center for unexcelled eating around the turn of the century and before that. The Rennert family insisted upon the strictest culinary standards. It was said that during the last years of the hotel's existence, when good help was hard to find, Mrs. Rennert herself would don an apron, go into the kitchen and take charge.

½ onion, chopped
2 tablespoons butter
¾ pound fresh lump crab
  meat from blue crabs
½ teaspoon salt
½ teaspoon cayenne
dash of Worcestershire sauce

1 teaspoon dry mustard
2 tablespoons chopped green
  pepper
½ cup Béchamel Sauce (see
  Index)
dry bread crumbs
butter

Preheat oven to 370°F. Have ready 4 cleaned crab shells or ramekins.

Sauté the onion in the butter. Add the crab meat, seasonings, green pepper and béchamel sauce. Mix well.

Pile crab mixture into shells, sprinkle with bread crumbs, dot with butter, and brown in the oven for 25 minutes.

4 servings

DELAWARE CRAB CAKES

1½ cups fresh blue claw crab
  meat
1½ cups milk
1 teaspoon grated onion
1 teaspoon salt
⅛ teaspoon pepper
1½ tablespoons butter

3 tablespoons flour
4 egg yolks, beaten (3 for
  mixture, 1 for breading)
1½ tablespoons cream
1 cup bread crumbs
2 cups bacon fat for frying

Remove bits of shell from crab meat and chop crab finely in a blender.

Simmer milk, onion, salt and pepper for 1 minute.

In a separate saucepan melt the butter, stir in the flour, and cook for 1 minute. Remove from heat and stir in half of the milk gradually with a wire whisk until well blended. Stir in remaining milk and bring sauce slowly to a simmer until thickened.

Stir in three quarters of the egg yolks, the cream and crab meat. Spread in an even layer on a platter and chill in the refrigerator for 1 hour or longer, until stiff enough to handle.

Form crab mixture into 12 patties. Roll patties in remaining egg yolk and then in the bread crumbs. Fry in fat heated to 375°F. until brown on all sides.

6 to 8 servings

EASTERN SHORE CRAB CAKES

1 pound freshly cooked crab
   meat from blue crabs
½ teaspoon dry mustard
2 tablespoons mayonnaise
1 egg, beaten
½ teaspoon salt

pinch of cayenne pepper
2 slices of bread, wet and
   squeezed out
4 tablespoons bread crumbs
   or cornmeal
bacon fat for frying

Combine the crab meat with the mustard, mayonnaise, egg, salt, cayenne and moistened bread. Shape into 4 cakes and roll in bread crumbs or cornmeal.

Heat fat in a heavy frying pan. Add the cakes and cook over moderate heat until brown on one side, then turn and brown on the other. Or fry the cakes in deep fat.

4 servings

NEW ORLEANS CRAB CAKES

1 tablespoon butter
1 onion, finely chopped
1 pound crab meat
1 garlic clove, minced
1 bay leaf, crushed
1 thyme sprig, chopped

2 parsley sprigs, chopped
pinch of cayenne
½ teaspoon salt
1 cup wet bread, squeezed out
lard

Melt the butter in a heavy skillet and sauté onion.

Mix together the crab meat, garlic, bay leaf, thyme, parsley, cayenne and salt. Stir into the skillet with the onion and add the moistened bread. Fry for about 3 minutes.

Remove from heat and cool. Form into 4 flat cakes and fry in hot lard until golden on both sides.

4 servings

CRAB CASSEROLE

4 tablespoons butter
½ cup chopped celery
2 tablespoons chopped green
    pepper
2 tablespoons flour
1 cup milk
1 egg yolk, beaten

2 tablespoons lemon juice
½ teaspoon salt
pinch of pepper
1 pound fresh crab meat (any
    kind)
¼ cup dry bread crumbs
2 tablespoons melted butter

Preheat oven to 350°F.

Melt the butter in a casserole. Cook celery and green pepper in butter until tender. Blend in flour, then gradually add milk, stirring, and cook over low heat until sauce is smooth and thickened.

Stir a little of the hot sauce into the egg yolk, then turn yolk mixture into the casserole, stirring constantly.

Add the lemon juice, seasonings and crab meat. Combine the bread crumbs and melted butter; sprinkle crumbs over the casserole. Bake for 20 to 25 minutes, or until brown.

6 servings

This recipe may be used also for lobster meat or shrimps.

SAUTÉED KING CRAB LEGS

24 frozen King crab legs
1 cup light cream
flour
2 tablespoons olive oil
4 tablespoons butter

2 tablespoons chopped
    parsley
2 teaspoons grated lemon
    rind
1 tablespoon chopped capers

Defrost the crab legs. Slit the shells with scissors, remove the meat, and cut into 4-inch pieces.

Soak the crab pieces in cream for about 15 minutes. Pat crab dry and roll in flour. Discard the cream.

Heat the oil in a heavy skillet and lightly brown the pieces on all sides. Transfer to a heated platter and keep warm.

In a small skillet melt the butter and stir in the parsley, lemon rind and capers. Pour over the crab legs.

4 servings

BAKED CRAB MEAT IN SHELLS

¼ pound butter
½ cup chopped onion
2 tablespoons flour
½ cup milk
½ cup tomato sauce
½ teaspoon salt

pinch of pepper
1 pound fresh crab meat (any kind)
¼ cup grated Cheddar cheese
½ cup soft bread crumbs

Preheat oven to 350°F. Have ready 6 well-greased shells or ramekins.

Melt the butter; cook onion in butter until tender. Blend in the flour and add the milk gradually, stirring; cook over low heat until sauce is smooth and thickened.

Add tomato sauce, seasonings and crab meat. Spoon into the shells or ramekins.

Combine the cheese and bread crumbs and sprinkle some over the top of each shell.

Bake for 20 minutes, or until brown.

6 servings

DEVILED KING CRAB LEGS

16 large frozen King crab legs
1 cup melted butter
2 cups bread crumbs
1 teaspoon Tabasco

1 teaspoon salt
½ teaspoon freshly ground pepper
1 teaspoon dry mustard

Defrost the crab legs. Slit the shells with scissors or a sharp knife. Brush with melted butter.

Combine remaining butter with the bread crumbs and seasonings and press the ribs into this mixture.

Broil 5 or 6 inches from the heat until brown and crisp.

4 servings

CRAB MEAT MORNAY

4 tablespoons butter
3 tablespoons flour
2 tablespoons cornstarch
1 cup Fish Stock (see Index)
1 cup milk
2 tablespoons heavy cream

½ teaspoon salt
½ teaspoon pepper
1 pound crab meat, cooked or
   canned
½ cup grated Parmesan
   cheese

Melt the butter, blend in the flour and cornstarch, and gradually stir in the stock. Simmer, stirring, for 5 minutes.

Gradually stir in the milk and then the cream and seasonings.

Add the crab meat and transfer to a 1½-quart casserole. Sprinkle with cheese and brown under the broiler.

6 servings

This recipe may be used also for lobster meat.

KING CRAB PIE

1 tablespoon butter
2 cups bread cubes
2 cups King crab meat, cut up
½ cup Mayonnaise (see Index)
1 onion, chopped
1 green pepper, chopped
1 cup chopped celery
1 teaspoon salt

½ teaspoon pepper
2 cups milk
3 eggs, beaten
1 cup Béchamel Sauce (see
   Index)
2 tablespoons grated
     Monterey Jack cheese
paprika

Butter a 3-quart casserole. Place half of the bread cubes in the bottom of the casserole. Mix together the crab, mayonnaise, onion, green pepper, celery and seasonings. Spoon over the bread cubes. Cover with remaining bread cubes.

Mix together the milk and eggs, and pour evenly over the top. Let stand for 1 hour.

Preheat oven to 350°F.

Spoon the béchamel sauce into the casserole. Do not stir. Cover with grated cheese, dust with paprika, and bake in the oven for 1 hour.

8 servings

This recipe may be used also for any other kind of crab meat.

DEVILED BLUE CRABS

1 pound freshly cooked crab
   meat from blue crabs
¼ teaspoon dry mustard
¼ teaspoon grated mace
pinch of cayenne
1 tablespoon chopped parsley

1 teaspoon Worcestershire
   sauce
3 tablespoons melted butter
1 tablespoon lemon juice
1 egg, beaten
¼ cup dry bread crumbs

Preheat oven to 350°F. Have ready 4 well-buttered shells or ramekins.

Add the seasonings to the crab meat. Stir in the melted butter, lemon juice and beaten egg.

Divide among the shells or ramekins, and sprinkle with bread crumbs. Bake in oven for 15 minutes, or until golden.

4 servings

FRIED SOFTSHELL CRABS

8 live softshell blue-claw crabs
2 eggs, beaten
¼ cup milk
2 teaspoons salt

½ cup flour
½ cup dry bread crumbs
cooking oil

Dress crabs by cutting off the faces just back of the eyes, lift the top shells at both points, and remove the gills and digestive organs. Remove the aprons. Rinse crabs in cold water.

Combine the eggs, milk and salt. Combine flour and crumbs.

Dip crabs into egg mixture, then into flour mixture. Fry crabs in ⅛ inch hot (but not smoking) cooking oil in a heavy skillet for 8 to 10 minutes, or until brown on both sides. Or fry in deep fat heated to 375°F. for 4 minutes.

4 servings

SOFTSHELL CRABS SAUTÉED IN BUTTER

8 live softshell crabs, or
   thawed frozen crabs
flour

½ teaspoon salt
4 tablespoons butter

Dress live crabs by cutting off the faces just behind the eyes. Lift the top shells at both points and remove the gills and digestive organs. Remove the aprons. Rinse crabs in cold water.

Sprinkle lightly with flour and salt. Sauté quickly on both sides in hot butter until golden.

4 servings

KING CRAB RÉMOULADE

1 cup Mayonnaise (see Index)
1 teaspoon lemon juice
3 tablespoons snipped chives
3 tablespoons minced parsley
Dijon mustard

1 pound King crab meat,
   fresh, thawed frozen or
   canned
buttered toast points

Put the mayonnaise, lemon juice, chives, parsley and mustard to taste in a mixing bowl. Beat well with a wire whisk. Let stand for 30 minutes.

Stir in the crab meat, and pile on toast points.

8 servings

This recipe may be used also for any other kind of crab meat.

NORFOLK CRAB SALAD

1 pound lump or backfin crab
   meat
1½ cups chopped celery
1 teaspoon Worcestershire
   sauce
dash of Tabasco

1 cup Mayonnaise (see Index)
lettuce
olive oil
1 tomato, sliced
1 hard-cooked egg, quartered

Mix together the crab, celery, Worcestershire, Tabasco and mayonnaise. Take care not to break up the crab lumps.

Wash the lettuce, dry thoroughly, and toss with olive oil. Arrange in a salad bowl, pile in the crab-meat mixture, and garnish with the tomato slices and egg quarters.

4 servings

This recipe may be used also for lobster and shrimps.

CRAB MEAT RAVIGOTE

1 pound fresh lump crab
   meat from blue crabs
2 tablespoons chopped sweet
   pickle
2 tablespoons lemon juice
1 hard-cooked egg, chopped
2 tablespoons chopped onion
1 tablespoon chopped parsley

¼ teaspoon salt
pinch of pepper
salad greens
¼ cup mayonnaise
2 tablespoons chopped
   stuffed olives
¼ teaspoon paprika
pimiento strips

Combine the first 8 ingredients, taking care not to break up the crab lumps. Place on a bed of salad greens.

Mix together the mayonnaise, olives and paprika, and pile on top of the crab mixture. Garnish with pimiento strips.

6 servings

This recipe may be used also for lobster meat or shrimps.

CRAB-MEAT CASSEROLE WITH CHEESE

6 tablespoons butter
4 tablespoons flour
¼ cup water
1 cup half-and-half
½ pound freshly cooked crab
   meat from blue crabs

¼ cup chopped green pepper
1 pimiento, chopped
2 hard-cooked eggs, chopped
1 teaspoon salt
½ cup bread crumbs
½ cup grated Cheddar cheese

Preheat oven to 350°F.

Melt 4 tablespoons butter, blend in the flour, stir in the water, then the half-and-half. Simmer, stirring, until sauce is smooth and thickened.

Add crab meat, green pepper, pimiento, eggs and salt. Stir carefully, to avoid breaking up the crab lumps.

Transfer to a buttered 1-quart casserole. Top with bread crumbs, dot with remaining butter, and sprinkle with cheese. Bake for 30 minutes, or until golden.

4 servings

This recipe may be used also for lobster meat.

CRAYFISHES

The crayfish is a small freshwater crustacean closely resembling the American lobster. There are many species found throughout the world in both cold and warm waters, in tiny streams and in rivers. Crayfishes (also spelled crawfishes) range greatly in size, with bodies measuring from 1 inch to 8 inches in length, but those measuring less than 3 inches are generally deemed too small for gastronomic consideration. These little creatures, known throughout western and midwestern states as "Crawdads," are sought out each spring by children as sport. Dangle a bit of food anywhere near a crawdad and it will grab it with its claws and thus is easily captured.

Crayfishes are a very popular food in many countries of Europe. Sweden, Norway, Denmark, Belgium and France all cultivate them in freshwater farms to satisfy their ever-increasing demands. In the United States they are found in varying quantities almost everywhere, but more plentifully in the extreme north and extreme south—in Louisiana and neighboring states, and in Oregon and Washington. A small town in the Louisiana Creole country, Breaux Bridge, claims for itself the title, *La Capitale Mondiale des Écrivisses,* where crayfishes are caught and served in every conceivable manner—fried, steamed, sautéed, stewed and gumboed.

Crayfish country throughout the United States experiences a mild sort of hysteria each spring, as crayfishermen, bushel baskets and dip nets in hand, invade streams, rills and creeks, turning over rocks and poking sticks into riverbed holes. But by far a more efficient way of catching the little crustaceans is to trap them in wire funnel traps baited with fish heads.

How to Buy

In the United States crayfishes are not always marketed in areas outside of their habitat. This is not because of any difficulty in shipping or storing, but only because the demand has not yet been developed. With the establishment of crayfish farms in Louisiana, Mississippi, Arkansas and other southern states, the consumption of crayfishes is expected to increase.

Where crayfishes are sold they usually appear live on ice, cooked in the shell, or frozen.

How to Prepare

If the crayfish is live, wash thoroughly under running water to remove grit. Place in boiling water and soak for 10 minutes. Remove the head, reserving the orange-colored fat. Remove meat from tail shell by slitting the covering with kitchen scissors. Peel off the shell and remove the intestinal vein running down the back.

How to Store

Live crayfishes will stay fresh for up to 2 weeks if kept on ice. Boiled crayfishes may be kept twice as long. In a frozen state they will last for a month or more.

BOILED CRAYFISHES

2 pounds crayfishes, fresh or
    frozen
2 quarts boiling water

2 tablespoons salt
1 teaspoon snipped fresh dill

Drop the crayfishes into the boiling water, add the seasonings, cover, and cook for 10 minutes, or until they turn bright red.

Drain and chill. Serve whole at cocktail time with a squeeze of lemon or a choice of sauces (see Index).

Or peel, remove head, claws and legs, and use in recipes given for shrimps or spiny lobsters.

4 to 6 servings

SKEWERED CRAYFISH TAILS

1 garlic clove, crushed
1 scallion, minced
2 teaspoons minced parsley
2 tablespoons olive oil

2 tablespoons butter
1 pound shelled cooked
    crayfish tails
8 slices of bacon, quartered

Preheat broiler to 400°F.

Sauté the garlic, scallion and parsley in the oil and butter. Do not brown.

Thread the crayfish tails and bacon slices alternately on skewers, and cook under the broiler until bacon is done, brushing with the garlic sauce from time to time.

4 servings

CRAYFISH BUSH

This is a celebrated Creole hors-d'oeuvre served at parties and social functions in and around New Orleans. Boiled crayfishes are presented as an elaborate table garnish. Stacked around and hung from a goblet of fresh celery, parsley and asparagus tips, they form a sort of bush. The red crayfish shells intermingling with the green colors of the vegetables make a most pleasing table centerpiece.

CRAYFISH SOUP

½ cup Fish Stock (see Index)
2 cups light cream
2 tablespoons butter
pinch of grated mace or
  nutmeg

pinch of salt
½ pound shelled cooked
  crayfish tails, chopped
2 teaspoons sherry wine
paprika

Heat the stock in a saucepan; stir in the cream, butter and seasonings, and simmer for 2 minutes.

Add the crayfish meat and sherry. Simmer for 2 minutes longer. Sprinkle with paprika.

4 servings

CRAYFISH BISQUE

24 crayfishes in the shell
1 tablespoon salt
½ cup finely chopped celery
½ cup minced onion
¼ pound butter
½ cup crumbled bread,
  soaked and squeezed dry
2 tablespoons minced parsley
⅛ teaspoon ground celery
  seed
1 teaspoon dried savory

1 egg yolk, beaten
1 tablespoon flour
1 garlic clove, minced
pinch of dried thyme
1 teaspoon Worcestershire
  sauce
dash of Tabasco
1 hot red pepper pod, seeded
1 cup dry white wine
salt and pepper
1 quart water

Cover the crayfishes with cold water, add the salt, and boil for 15 minutes. Cool.

Slice off the heads and clean the heads, scraping insides of shells. Set aside for stuffing. Chop the tail meat and reserve.

Sauté the celery and half of the onion in half of the butter for 2 minutes. Add half of the tail meat, the soaked bread, 1 tablespoon of the parsley, the celery seed, savory and egg yolk. Mix well, stuff into the head shells, and reserve.

Melt remaining butter and sauté the rest of the onion for 2 minutes. Blend in the flour and cook until browned. Add remaining chopped tail meat and all the other ingredients. Stir, cover, and simmer for about 1 hour. Add the stuffed crayfish heads, heat briefly, and serve.

4 servings

CRAYFISH BROIL

1 garlic clove, cut
6 tablespoons melted butter
1½ pounds shelled cooked
    crayfish tails
½ teaspoon salt
½ teaspoon white pepper
few grains of cayenne
flour
paprika

Preheat broiler to 400°F.

Rub the bottom and sides of a shallow baking dish with garlic. Add half of the melted butter and swish it around.

Arrange the crayfish tails in the dish; season with salt, pepper and cayenne. Dust lightly with flour and paprika. Pour on the remaining butter.

Cook under the broiler for 10 minutes, or until golden.

4 servings

This recipe may be used also for shrimps and lobsterettes.

CRAYFISH NANTUA

2 pounds crayfishes (about
    36), fresh or frozen
2 cups Fish Stock (see Index)
2 tablespoons butter
1 tablespoon finely chopped
    shallot
½ teaspoon salt
few grains of cayenne
1 tablespoon Cognac, warmed
½ cup Sauce Nantua (see
    Index)
½ cup Hollandaise Sauce (see
    Index)

Drop the crayfishes into a pot with the fish stock, cover, and steam over high heat for 5 minutes, or until crayfishes turn red. Remove and let them cool. Slit the shells; remove the meat.

In a heavy skillet, heat the butter; add the shallot, salt, cayenne and the crayfish tails; cook until crayfishes are cooked through. Add the warmed Cognac, ignite, and stir until flames die.

Preheat broiler.

Stir in sauce Nantua and heat until bubbly. Remove skillet from the heat and gradually stir in the Hollandaise sauce.

Divide the mixture into 4 gratin dishes and brown under the broiler for 1 minute.

4 servings

CRAYFISH TAILS, BAYOU STYLE

2 tablespoons butter
1 tablespoon flour
1 cup Fish Stock (see Index)
1 cup cream
2 egg yolks, beaten
1 tablespoon chili sauce
½ teaspoon salt

few grains of cayenne
2 teaspoons minced onion
1½ pounds shelled cooked
    crayfish tails
dry bread crumbs
butter for topping

Preheat oven to 375°F. Have ready 6 buttered ramekins.

Melt the butter; stir in the flour, then the stock and cream. Simmer for 5 minutes. Remove sauce from the heat and cool.

Stir in the egg yolks, chili sauce, seasonings and onion. Add the crayfish tails, stir, and transfer to the ramekins.

Sprinkle with bread crumbs, dot with butter, and brown in the oven.

6 servings

This recipe may be used also for shrimps and lobsterettes.

CURRIED CRAYFISH PIE

3 slices of bread, crusts
    trimmed
1 cup milk
3 tablespoons melted butter
1 teaspoon Worcestershire
    sauce

1 tablespoon curry powder
pinch of ground ginger
½ teaspoon salt
½ teaspoon white pepper
1½ pounds shelled cooked
    crayfish tails

Preheat oven to 375°F.

Soak the bread in the milk and mash with a fork. Add the butter, Worcestershire, seasonings and crayfish tails.

Transfer to a buttered 4-cup casserole or 9-inch pie dish. Bake in the oven for 20 minutes.

4 servings

This recipe may be used also for shrimps or spiny lobsters.

CRAYFISHES AU GRATIN

4 tablespoons butter
4 tablespoons flour
1 cup Fish Stock (see Index)
1 cup cream
1½ pounds shelled cooked
    crayfish tails

1 cup grated cheese
½ teaspoon salt
½ teaspoon white pepper

Preheat oven to 375°F.

Melt the butter in a saucepan; stir in the flour and cook for 1 minute.

Mix stock and cream together and stir into the flour mixture; cook over low heat until sauce is smooth and thickened.

Add the crayfish tails, half of the cheese and the seasonings. Place in a shallow 6-cup baking dish and sprinkle with remaining cheese. Bake in the oven until brown.

4 servings

This recipe may be used also for shrimps and lobsterettes.

OLD-FASHIONED CRAYFISH SALAD

2 pounds crayfishes, fresh or
    frozen
2 quarts boiling water
salt
1 cup finely chopped celery
2 tablespoons olive oil
½ teaspoon lemon juice

¼ teaspoon pepper
½ cup Mayonnaise (see
    Index)
1 small head of Boston
    lettuce, washed and dried
1 pimiento, cut into julienne
    strips

Drop the crayfishes into the boiling water with 2 tablespoons salt. Cook for 5 minutes, or until they turn red. Remove crayfishes and let them cool. Slit the tails, and remove the meat.

Mix together the crayfish meat, celery, oil, lemon juice, ¼ teaspoon salt, the pepper and mayonnaise. Spoon onto the lettuce leaves and garnish with pimiento strips.

4 servings

This recipe may be used also for lobster meat, crab meat, shrimps or almost any other shellfishes.

CRAYFISH TAILS AU BEURRE NOIR

¼ pound butter
1 teaspoon lemon juice
1½ pounds shelled cooked
   crayfish tails

½ teaspoon salt
½ teaspoon pepper
minced parsley

Melt the butter in a heavy skillet and cook over low heat until dark brown. Add lemon juice, crayfish tails, salt and pepper.

Turn the crayfish tails once. Serve garnished with parsley.

4 servings

This recipe may be used also for shrimps and lobsterettes.

CRAYFISHES IN ASPIC

2 pounds crayfishes, fresh or
   frozen
2 quarts boiling water
salt
4 cups Chicken Stock (see
   Index)
2 tablespoons finely chopped
   onion

2 envelopes unflavored
   gelatin, softened in ½ cup
   warm water
2 cups finely chopped celery
2 tablespoons lemon juice
lettuce leaves
sour cream

Drop the crayfishes into the boiling water with 2 tablespoons salt. Cook for 5 minutes, or until they turn red. Remove crayfishes and let them cool. Slit the tails, remove the meat, and reserve it.

Bring the chicken stock to a boil; add the onion and cook for 2 minutes. Remove from heat and cool to lukewarm. Stir in the softened gelatin until dissolved. Mix in celery, lemon juice, ½ teaspoon salt and reserved crayfish tails.

Pour into a 2-quart mold and chill for 4 hours. Unmold, and serve on lettuce leaves, topped with sour cream.

6 servings

This recipe may be used also for lobster meat, crab meat, shrimps or almost any other shellfishes.

AMERICAN LOBSTERS

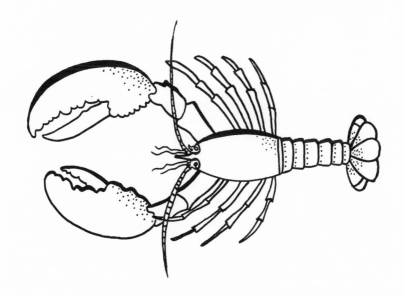

The American Lobster, sometimes called the Maine Lobster, is found in the cold waters of the North Atlantic from Newfoundland to as far south as North Carolina. Usually weighing from 1 to 5 pounds, it is occasionally found up to 45 pounds or more. Visually, this lobster is characterized by two large claws—the larger and heavier "crusher" and the "quick" claw, sharper and more pointed, used for fighting and biting.

American Lobsters are trapped commercially, predominantly off the Maine coast, at depths up to 200 feet. The minimum legal length—$3^3/_{16}$ inches measuring the carapace only—is attained in 7 or 8 years of development from the larva stage. In the warmer

New Jersey waters lobsters grow faster, and larger. There has long been talk of developing lobster farms here to increase the ever-dwindling supply.

The European side of the Atlantic yields a similar clawed lobster, but in far smaller quantities.

There are also smaller members of the big-claw family found on both sides of the Atlantic, generally classified as Lobsterettes. These include the Dublin Bay prawn, the Langoustine, the Italian Scampo and the Lobsterettes of Denmark and Norway. Along the American coast there are the West Indian or Caribbean and the Florida Lobsterettes, the latter found as far north as New Jersey.

How to Buy

American Lobsters are found in the market in 4 sizes: Chicken Lobsters (about 1 pound), Medium (1 to 1½ pounds), Large (1½ to 2½ pounds), and Jumbos (about 4 pounds), the average size being 1½ pounds and the largest ever caught being 42 pounds. (Tenderness of meat has nothing to do with size of lobster.) The best lobsters in the market are those kept on ice, not the ones in a tank which usually have absorbed several ounces of water. Of course your purchase must be live. The legs should move and its tail should curl under when it is picked up.

Lobster meat picked from the shell is packed in cans and sold frozen, pasteurized and smoked.

How to Prepare

a. Place live lobster on its back. Insert a sharp knife between body shell and tail, and cut down quickly to sever spinal cord. Or plunge head first into a large pot of boiling salted water (1 tablespoon salt to 1 quart water) for 7 minutes if less than 2 pounds, or 10 minutes if 2 pounds or more.*
b. With a sharp knife split lobster open along back from head to tail.
c. Remove black vein running from head to tail, and small sac behind head.

*Or place lobsters in cold water and bring water to a boil. Scientific experiments made to ascertain which is the more humane way to kill a lobster revealed the following surprising results: lobsters placed in cold water appeared to expire gradually and painlessly as the temperature of the water increased, while those plunged alive into boiling water made violent attempts to escape, remaining alive up to a full minute.

Lobster is now ready to use in any recipe you wish to select. Or it is ready to eat as-is, hot or cold. There is little waste. The green tomalley (liver) has a delicious delicate flavor, as has the pink roe or coral. The shells may be ground up or pounded into powder for use in flavoring sauces, lobster bisque, etc.

How to Store

Live lobsters should be stored in the coldest part of the refrigerator, and for only a few hours. Do not keep them in water. Frozen lobsters and the meat or parts of lobsters will keep for almost any reasonable length of time but, once thawed, should be used the same day. Refreezing can be done safely within a short time after thawing, but only at a sacrifice in flavor.

BOILED LOBSTERS

4 live lobsters, 1½ pounds
    each
4 quarts boiling water
6 tablespoons salt

melted butter or Drawn
    Butter (see Index)
lemon wedges

Plunge lobsters head first, one at a time, into the boiling salted water. Cover and cook for 8 to 10 minutes, or until shells are red. Drain.

Place lobsters on their backs, cut lengthwise into halves, and remove the stomachs (just behind head) and the black intestinal veins.

Serve hot with melted or drawn butter or cold with mayonnaise or other dressing (see Index), lemon wedges on the side.

4 servings

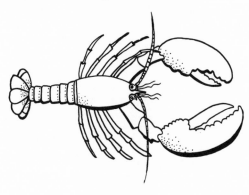

BROILED LOBSTERS

4 live lobsters, 1½ pounds
    each
6 tablespoons melted butter
½ teaspoon salt
½ teaspoon white pepper

½ teaspoon paprika
lemon wedges
melted butter or Drawn
    Butter (see Index)

Kill the lobsters by inserting the point of a sharp knife between the body and the tail sections.

Place lobsters on their backs, cut lengthwise into halves, and remove the stomachs (just behind the heads) and the black intestinal veins. Crack the claws.

Arrange in a broiling pan, cut side up. Brush with butter and sprinkle with salt, pepper and paprika.

Broil about 4 inches from the source of heat for 12 to 15 minutes, or until lightly browned. Baste with butter once during broiling.

Garnish with lemon wedges and serve with melted or drawn butter.

4 servings

LOBSTER SPREAD

1 cup finely chopped lobster
    meat, fresh, thawed
    frozen or canned
4 hard-cooked egg yolks,
    mashed
4 tablespoons heavy cream,
    sweet or sour

½ teaspoon Worcestershire
    sauce
1 teaspoon dry mustard
½ teaspoon salt
toast squares

Mix first 6 ingredients together. Check seasoning. Serve on toast squares.

4 servings

This recipe may be used also for crab meat or shrimps.

HOT LOBSTER CANAPÉS

1 cup chopped lobster meat,
    fresh, thawed frozen or
    canned
6 ripe olives, chopped
1 teaspoon chopped capers
2 tablespoons heavy cream,
    sweet or sour

½ teaspoon salt
½ teaspoon pepper
dash of Worcestershire sauce
toast squares

Mix first 7 ingredients together and spread on toast squares. Brown under the broiler for a moment and serve hot.

24 canapés

This recipe may be used also for crab meat or chopped shrimps.

LOBSTER SOUP

3 tablespoons butter
½ cup chopped mushrooms,
    fresh or canned
1 onion, chopped
1 tablespoon chopped parsley
1 garlic clove, crushed
1 bay leaf
½ teaspoon ground allspice
½ cup minced cooked ham
1 teaspoon salt

1 tablespoon butter creamed
    with 1 tablespoon flour
½ cup canned tomatoes
1 cup Fish Stock (see index)
1 cup hot water
2 hard-cooked eggs, chopped
½ pound lobster meat,
    coarsely chopped
2 tablespoons sherry wine

Melt the butter in a large pot. Stir in the mushrooms, onion, parsley, garlic, bay leaf, allspice, ham and salt. Cook over low heat for 5 minutes.

Stir in the butter-flour mixture (*beurre manié*), then the tomatoes, stock and water. Cover and simmer for 15 minutes.

Add the chopped eggs and lobster meat, stir in the wine, and serve.

4 servings

HOT LOBSTER BALLS

2 tablespoons butter
1 tablespoon chopped scallion
2 tablespoons flour
½ cup cream
1 cup minced lobster meat

dash of Worcestershire sauce
dash of Tabasco
½ teaspoon salt
cooking oil
dry bread crumbs

Melt the butter in a heavy skillet; sauté the scallion in butter for 1 minute. Stir in the flour, then the cream to make a smooth, thick sauce.

Stir in the lobster meat and seasonings. Remove from the heat and let cool.

Heat the oil to 400°F. in a heavy skillet. Drop the lobster mixture by the teaspoon into bread crumbs. Roll to coat evenly. Fry a few at a time in the hot oil until golden.

about 40 balls

This recipe may be used also for crab meat.

LOBSTER BISQUE

3 tablespoons butter
1 tablespoon minced onion
1 teaspoon minced parsley
2 tablespoons flour
1 tablespoon powdered
    lobster shell
½ teaspoon dried thyme
1 teaspoon salt

¼ teaspoon pepper
few grains of cayenne
1½ cups minced freshly
    cooked lobster meat
2 cups Chicken Stock or Fish
    Stock (see Index)
2 cups light cream
½ cup dry sherry wine

Melt the butter in a heavy pot. Stir in the onion and parsley and cook slowly until onion is light brown.

Stir in the flour until mixture thickens.

Add the powdered shell, seasonings and lobster meat, and cook for 5 minutes, stirring.

Stir in the stock and cook for 15 minutes longer.

Remove from heat. Stir in the cream and sherry. Serve in cups.

6 servings

LOBSTER GUMBO

3 tablespoons butter
1 onion, chopped
1 garlic clove, crushed
1 celery rib, chopped
1 tomato, peeled and chopped
1 cup sliced okra, fresh,
    canned or thawed frozen

1 bay leaf
pinch of dried thyme
few dashes of Tabasco
½ teaspoon salt
¼ teaspoon pepper
1 quart boiling water
½ pound lobster meat,
    coarsely chopped

Melt the butter in a heavy pot. Sauté onion, garlic and celery in the butter for about 10 minutes.

Add tomato, okra and seasonings. Stir in the boiling water, cover, and simmer for 30 minutes. Remove the bay leaf.

Add lobster meat, and continue simmering for 3 minutes. Serve with rice.

4 servings

This recipe may be used also for crab meat.

LOBSTER CHOWDER

½ pound salt pork, diced
2 tablespoons flour
pinch of grated mace
pinch of cayenne
1 teaspoon salt
3 cups milk

1 cup cream
2 tablespoons butter
1 pound lobster meat,
    coarsely chopped
paprika

Sauté the salt pork in a large pot until light brown. Blend in the flour and seasonings and cook for 2 or 3 minutes.

Stir in the milk, cream and butter, and simmer until soup is smooth and thickened.

Add the lobster and simmer for 5 minutes. Serve sprinkled with paprika.

6 servings

BAKED STUFFED LOBSTER

4 live lobsters, 1½ pounds
   each
3 cups soft bread cubes

4 tablespoons melted butter
2 tablespoons grated onion
1 garlic clove, minced

Boil and clean the lobsters; remove and reserve the green liver and coral.

Preheat oven to 400°F.

Mix together the bread cubes, butter, onion, garlic, liver and coral. Place this stuffing in the body cavities and spread over the tail meat.

Place lobsters in a shallow baking pan, stuffing side up, and bake for about 20 minutes, or until golden.

4 servings

VARIATION: Add a cup of grated cheese to the dressing.

LOBSTER CROQUETTES

6 tablespoons butter
6 tablespoons flour
1 teaspoon salt
dash of pepper
1 cup milk
1 teaspoon lemon juice
2 cups chopped cooked
   lobster meat

fat for deep-frying
dry bread crumbs
1 egg, lightly beaten with 2
   tablespoons water
few grains of cayenne
1 cup half milk, half cream
1 cup chopped green olives

Melt 4 tablespoons butter over very low heat and stir in 4 table-spoons flour, ½ teaspoon salt and a dash of pepper until smooth. Gradually stir in the milk and simmer over low heat until mixture thickens.

Add the lemon juice and lobster meat. Mix and chill.

Heat the fat to 390°F.

Form the lobster mixture into croquettes. Roll croquettes in bread crumbs, then in the egg mixture, then in bread crumbs again.

Fry the croquettes a few at a time until golden.

Meanwhile, melt remaining 2 tablespoons butter, stir in remaining

2 tablespoons flour, ½ teaspoon salt and a little cayenne, then the half-and-half. Continue stirring over heat until mixture is smooth and thickened. Stir in the chopped olives and pour over the croquettes.

4 servings

This recipe may be used also for crab meat.

LOBSTER NEWBURG

Originally, Lobster Newburg was called Lobster à la Wenberg after Ben Wenberg, a sea captain and gourmet who took most of his meals at Delmonico's in New York. He is said to have invented this method of preparing lobster. Charles Delmonico and the Captain had a falling out and Delmonico changed the name of this, his most popular offering, to Newburg (*new* being *wen* spelled backwards). Or so goes the story. In any event, the original recipe is as follows:

4 lobsters, 1¼ pounds each	1 cup Madeira or sherry wine,
1 tablespoon sweet butter	warmed
1 teaspoon salt	1 cup heavy cream
½ teaspoon white pepper	3 egg yolks
few grains of cayenne	

Plunge the lobsters, head first, into boiling salted water and cook for 15 minutes, or until shells turn pink. Cool. Crack the claws, split the carcass lengthwise, and remove and discard the black intestinal vein. Remove and reserve the coral and tomalley. Remove the meat from the claws and tail, and cut into ½-inch slices.

Melt the butter and sauté the lobster pieces for a few minutes, or until pink. Add the salt, pepper, cayenne and wine. Simmer for 3 minutes.

Add half of the cream, the tomalley and coral, and simmer for 3 minutes longer.

Remove from the heat and stir in the remaining cream blended with the egg yolks. Heat gently, but do not boil. Serve on toast or in individual ramekins.

4 servings

This recipe may be used also for crab meat.

LOBSTER À L'AMÉRICAINE

2 live lobsters, 2 pounds each
¼ cup olive oil
3 tablespoons finely chopped
  shallots or scallions
1 garlic clove, finely chopped
4 fresh tomatoes, peeled and
  quartered
2 tablespoons chopped
  parsley

1 tablespoon chopped fresh
  tarragon
½ teaspoon salt
few grains of cayenne
1 cup Fish Stock (see Index)
½ cup dry white wine
¼ cup Cognac, warmed

Kill the lobsters by cutting quickly between the body and tail. Remove and discard the legs. Crack the claws. Split the carcasses lengthwise, removing and discarding the black intestinal vein and the gritty substance behind the head. Remove and reserve the tomalley and coral. Cut the lobsters, shells and all, into 1½-inch pieces.

Heat the oil in a heavy skillet and sauté the shallots and garlic for 2 minutes. Add the tomatoes, parsley, tarragon, seasonings, stock and wine. Cover and simmer for 20 minutes.

Pour the Cognac over the lobster pieces, ignite it, then add the sauce. Cook for 15 minutes longer.

Just before serving, add the reserved tomalley and coral.

4 servings

SCALLOPED LOBSTER

2 tablespoons butter
2 tablespoons flour
1 teaspoon salt
½ teaspoon pepper
½ teaspoon paprika
1 cup Fish Stock or Chicken
  Stock (see Index)
½ cup cream

2 egg yolks, beaten
3 cups cut-up cooked fresh
  lobster meat
½ cup sherry wine
bread crumbs
butter for topping

Preheat oven to 400°F.

Heat the butter in a heavy skillet. Stir in the flour and seasonings, then the stock, and simmer over low heat until sauce is smooth and thickened.

Stir in the cream and egg yolks. Do not let the sauce boil.

Mix in the lobster pieces and stir in the sherry.

Transfer to a buttered casserole, dust with bread crumbs, dot with butter, and brown in the oven.

4 servings

This recipe may be used also for crab meat.

LOBSTER CANTONESE

2 live lobsters, 2 pounds each
1 tablespoon oil
1 pound lean pork, ground
1 garlic clove, minced
½ teaspoon pepper
1 cup Fish Stock (see Index)

2 eggs, beaten
2 tablespoons cornstarch
   dissolved in ¼ cup water
1 tablespoon soy sauce
¼ cup dry sherry wine

Kill the lobsters by inserting the point of a sharp knife between the body and tail. Remove and crack the claws. Remove and discard the legs. Split the bodies lengthwise and remove the black intestinal vein and the sac behind the head. Cut the lobster halves, still in shells, each into 3 pieces.

Heat the oil in a heavy skillet and sauté the pork, garlic and pepper until pork is brown.

Add the lobster pieces and stock; cover and cook over high heat for 5 minutes.

Mix together the eggs, cornstarch mixture, soy sauce and sherry, and stir into the skillet. Cook for 5 minutes longer.

4 servings

LOBSTER FRA DIAVOLO

2 live lobsters, 2 pounds each
½ cup olive oil
½ cup minced parsley
1 teaspoon crumbled dried
    orégano
1 onion, finely chopped

1 garlic clove, minced
1 teaspoon salt
½ teaspoon freshly ground
    pepper
2 cups chopped cooked
    tomatoes
¼ cup Cognac, warmed

Plunge the lobsters head first into boiling water for 2 minutes. Crack the claws, split the bodies lengthwise into halves, and remove and discard the black intestinal veins and the head sacs. Remove and reserve the tomalley and coral.

Mix together the tomalley, coral and ¼ cup oil. Stir in the parsley, orégano, onion, garlic, salt, pepper and tomatoes. Simmer for 10 minutes.

Place the lobsters, cut side up, on a broiler pan and brush liberally with oil. Cook under the broiler for 3 minutes.

Spoon the sauce over the lobsters and continue cooking for 5 minutes longer.

Remove from the heat. Just before serving ignite the Cognac and pour it over the lobsters.

4 servings

STONINGTON LOBSTER PIE

6 tablespoons butter
¼ cup sherry wine
2 cups cut-up cooked lobster
    meat
2 tablespoons flour
¾ cup light cream mixed with
    2 lightly beaten egg yolks

¼ cup cracker crumbs mixed
    with ½ teaspoon paprika
2 tablespoons grated mild
    Cheddar cheese

Melt 2 tablespoons butter; stir in the sherry and lobster meat, and set aside.

Melt 3 tablespoons butter, stir in the flour, and cook for 1 minute.

Remove from the heat and stir in the cream and egg-yolk mixture.

Add the lobster meat and wine to the sauce and stir over low heat until smooth and thickened. Do not allow the sauce to boil.

Preheat oven to 300°F.

Transfer lobster mixture to a deep-dish pie plate. Sprinkle with the cracker-crumb mixture, top with grated cheese, and dot with remaining butter. Bake, uncovered, for 10 minutes, or until browned.

4 servings

LOBSTER EN BELLEVUE PARISIENNE

1 envelope unflavored gelatin
1¾ cups Fish Stock (see
    Index), simmering
1 live lobster, 3 pounds
salt
½ cup dry bread crumbs
1 to 2 cups Mayonnaise (see
    Index)

4 large romaine lettuce leaves
2 tablespoons olive oil
1 teaspoon vinegar
2 hard-cooked eggs, peeled
    and sliced
8 large pitted ripe olives,
    sliced into rings

Soften the gelatin in ¼ cup warm water, then dissolve it in the hot fish stock. Chill the aspic.

Plunge the lobster head first into boiling salted water to cover, cover the pot, and cook for 20 minutes. Remove lobster from water and let cool.

Remove the claws and legs from the lobster and place it on its back; slit from head to tail, taking care not to break the shell. Remove and discard the black intestinal vein and the spongelike organs. Remove the tail meat in one piece, slice into ½-inch medallions, and chill. Clean and chill the shell.

Crack the claws; remove and chop the meat. Pick out the leg and body meat, chop, and add to the claw meat; mix together with the bread crumbs and enough of the mayonnaise to bind; chill.

Wash and dry the lettuce leaves and toss with the oil and vinegar; Arrange on a 10-inch platter: place the lobster shell in the center, open side down, and arrange the chopped lobster meat and the egg slices around the sides. Lay the lobster medallions in an overlapping column on top of the shell. Place an olive ring in the center of each medallion and each egg slice.

Dab each of the egg slices with a bit of the mayonnaise and brush them and the medallions liberally with the chilled aspic, which should be on the point of setting, but not yet congealed. Chill the entire dish. Serve with the remaining mayonnaise in a sauceboat on the side.

4 servings

LOBSTER SALAD

8 crisp lettuce leaves
4 tablespoons olive oil
½ tablespoon vinegar
½ teaspoon salt
1 pound cooked lobster meat,
    diced

Mayonnaise or other dressing
    (see Index)
1 lemon, quartered

Wash the lettuce and dry thoroughly with a cloth towel. Toss well with the oil, vinegar and salt.

Arrange lettuce on 4 chilled salad plates. Pile lobster pieces on the lettuce. Top with dressing and serve with lemon wedges.

4 servings

This recipe may be used also for crab meat or shrimps.

SPINY
LOBSTERS

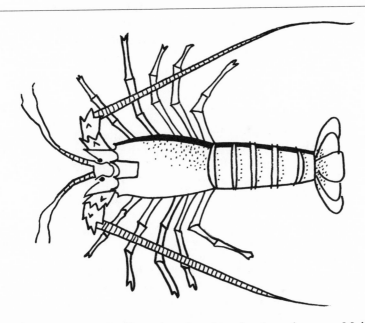

The Spiny Lobster is distantly related to the American, or Maine, lobster, but is of a different species entirely. Measuring from 8 to 16 inches from nose to tail, the Spiny has a carapace covered with sharp nodules or spines. While it lacks the handsome claws sported by its cousin, the Spiny does possess a set of miniscule claws which it uses for stuffing food into its mouth.

Spiny lobsters display a variegated color pattern ranging from reds to browns to yellows to blues, depending upon the habitat. Experts, it is said, can tell where a spiny comes from by its coloration and the formation of its nodules.

Spiny lobsters, commercially called Rock Lobsters, live in tropical and subtropical waters all over the world, walking about on the ocean floor in search of food. Those reaching American markets come principally from South Africa, Australia, New Zealand, and Chile, but they thrive also in the waters of the western Atlantic from North Carolina to the Caribbean and in the Gulf of Mexico. In the Pacific they can be found from northern California to Baja.

How to Buy

Almost all the Spiny lobsters gathered commercially are processed at sea as they are caught. The heads and legs are removed and the tails cleaned and quickly frozen—sometimes even packaged—before the fishing boats reach shore. In the stores they are sold by the pound, the tails weighing from 4 ounces to more than 2 pounds each. Allow ½ to ¾ pound per serving.

How to Prepare

Rock Lobster tails can be boiled, steamed, deep-fried or broiled. Or the raw meat can be removed from the shell before cooking. Baking should be avoided, because it toughens the meat beyond belief. Fast, brief cooking is strictly advised to preserve tenderness and flavor. If the tails are cooked in the shell, they should be split lengthwise through the center *before*—repeat, before—cooking. Otherwise, the meat will be extracted only with the greatest difficulty.

A broiled or boiled tail can be served whole by trimming off the shell while raw. You might wish, on occasions, to leave the fan attached to the meat. Small lobster tails can thus be deep-fried like tempura shrimps.

Almost any of the recipes given here for American lobsters may be successfully followed in preparing Rock Lobster tails.

How to Store

Since all Rock Lobster tails are marketed in a frozen state, they will keep (in the freezer, of course) almost indefinitely. Once thawed, however, they should be put to use within a few days. Refreezing, if not too long after thawing, is safe, but there will be a loss of flavor.

CURRIED LOBSTER CUBES

2½ pounds frozen lobster
    tails, thawed, shelled, and
    cut into cubes
½ teaspoon salt

½ teaspoon pepper
1 teaspoon curry powder
2 tablespoons butter
minced parsley

Season the lobster pieces with salt, pepper and curry powder.

Sauté pieces in hot butter. Sprinkle with parsley and serve hot on toothpicks.

4 servings

This recipe may be used also for shrimps.

LOBSTER TAILS IN SHERRY SAUCE

4 frozen lobster tails, ½
    pound each, thawed
2 tablespoons butter
1 tablespoon olive oil
1 tablespoon minced shallot

4 tablespoons chopped
    parsley
½ teaspoon salt
few grains of cayenne
¼ cup sherry wine
1 tablespoon lemon juice

Split the lobster tails vertically down the middle, but do not cut through. Drop into salted boiling water and cook for 8 minutes. Transfer to 4 heated ramekins and keep warm.

Heat the butter and oil and sauté the shallot slowly until translucent. Stir in the parsley, seasonings, sherry and lemon juice. Heat for a few minutes and spoon evenly over the lobster tails.

4 servings

LOBSTER HOLLANDAISE

3 frozen lobster tails, ½
    pound each, thawed
¼ pound butter
¼ cup Cognac, warmed
¼ cup dry white wine
½ cup heavy cream

1 teaspoon salt
½ teaspoon white pepper
1 cup Hollandaise Sauce (see
    Index)
bread crumbs

Preheat broiler to 400°F.

Remove lobster meat from the shells, and dice it. Sauté pieces in hot butter for 3 minutes.

Pour the Cognac over the lobster meat and ignite it.

Stir in the wine, cream and seasonings. Cook over low heat for a few minutes. Transfer to a buttered, heated 6-cup casserole.

Spoon on the Hollandaise, sprinkle with bread crumbs, and brown under the broiler.

4 servings

This recipe may be used also for shrimps.

LOBSTER THERMIDOR

½ cup melted butter
1 cup chopped fresh
   mushrooms
4 frozen lobster tails, ½ pound
   each, thawed
½ teaspoon salt
½ teaspoon freshly ground
   pepper
1 teaspoon dry mustard
1 tablespoon Worcestershire
   sauce

few grains of cayenne
½ cup dry sherry wine
¼ cup Cognac
1½ cups heavy cream
3 egg yolks, beaten
½ cup dry bread crumbs
½ cup grated Parmesan
   cheese
paprika

Preheat oven to 400°F.

Heat ¼ cup butter in a heavy skillet and sauté the mushrooms for 2 minutes. Remove from heat.

Remove lobster meat from the shells, cut into ½-inch pieces, and add to the skillet. Clean and reserve the shells.

Add the seasonings, sherry, Cognac, cream, egg yolks and bread crumbs to the skillet. Mix well.

Fill the lobster shells evenly with the stuffing. Brush with remaining butter, dust with cheese and paprika, and place in a shallow baking pan, shell side down.

Bake in the oven for 10 minutes, or until golden brown.

4 servings

This recipe may be used also for American lobsters.

CURRIED CREAMED LOBSTER TAILS

¼ pound butter
2 tablespoons minced shallots
½ garlic clove, minced
3 frozen lobster tails, ½
    pound each, thawed

2 eggs, beaten
½ cup heavy cream
2 teaspoons curry powder
toast squares
1 tablespoon minced parsley

Melt the butter in a heavy skillet; sauté shallots and garlic in butter for 2 minutes.

Remove lobster meat from the shells, dice, and add to the skillet. Sauté for 3 minutes.

Mix together the eggs, cream and curry powder and stir into the skillet. Heat thoroughly, but do not boil. Serve on toast squares, garnished with parsley.

4 servings

LOBSTER TAILS WITH TARRAGON

4 frozen lobster tails, ½
    pound each, thawed
½ cup fine bread crumbs
4 tablespoons butter, softened
1 tablespoon dried tarragon

¼ cup heavy cream
½ teaspoon salt
¼ teaspoon white pepper
2 tablespoons olive oil
1 tablespoon minced parsley

Preheat broiler to 350°F.

Remove lobster meat from the shells, and chop it. Reserve the shells. Mix meat with the crumbs, butter, tarragon, cream, salt and pepper.

Spoon this mixture into the lobster shells. Brush with oil and place on a baking sheet. Slide under the broiler and cook for about 8 minutes, or until golden brown. Sprinkle with minced parsley.

4 servings

LOBSTER MOUSSE

2 frozen lobster tails, ½
  pound each, thawed
1¼ cups chopped onions
¼ cup chopped shallots
1 envelope unflavored gelatin
  dissolved in ¼ cup hot
  water
¼ cup Mayonnaise (see
  Index)

1 tablespoon lemon juice
½ teaspoon salt
½ teaspoon freshly ground
  pepper
few grains of cayenne
½ teaspoon dry mustard
½ cup unsweetened whipped
  cream
minced parsley

Remove lobster meat from the shells and cut into pieces. Cook in simmering water until opaque. Mix with the onions and shallots and put through a food processor or meat grinder.

Blend in the gelatin, mayonnaise, lemon juice and seasonings. Fold in the whipped cream.

Spoon the mousse into a 1-quart mold, cover, and refrigerate for 3 to 4 hours, or until well set.

Dip the mold into hot water, turn upside down, and carefully unmold. Garnish with parsley.

4 servings

This recipe may be used also for crab meat.

SHRIMPS

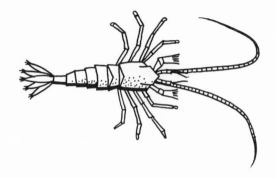

Shrimps are probably the most popular shellfish in the world—certainly in the United States where seafood lovers can't seem to get enough of them.

These little decapod marine crustaceans, varying so widely in size and color, constitute an industry of major importance in all of the waters surrounding America, from Alaska to the Gulf of Mexico. In Pacific waters alone there are almost a dozen species, and in the Atlantic, another dozen; pink, brown, white, royal red, spotted and striped. But only a professional can actually distinguish one from another.

The important difference, commercially, in shrimps is in their size, which usually varies from 3 to 5 inches in length. But there is a species found in the Aleutian Islands and the waters around Alaska that is so small as to require 150 or more to make a pound. And there is a variety found along the Atlantic Continental Shelf and in the depths of the Gulf of Mexico that measures up to 6 inches in length. These latter, according to a story, were discovered by a small-boat fisherman who, his motor having gone dead at the end of the day, was required to drift about through the night until daylight when rescue appeared. With nothing else to do, he fished—and came up with enormous shrimps that at night rose to the surface to feed, returning at daybreak to the 100-fathom depths of the Gulf beyond the reach of commercial shrimpers.

Even all the shrimps in United States waters are insufficient to satisfy American appetites. To augment our native supply, shrimp boats venture out of Texas and Florida to fish the waters of Mexico, the Caribbean and South America. Shrimp farms have sprung up in Louisiana, Arkansas and Texas; experiments are in full operation to cultivate shrimps by inducing fertilized females to spawn in saltwater ponds where the young can be nurtured until they reach marketable size. Other methods, some borrowed from the Japanese, are being avidly investigated, and there is hope that before long a successful and efficient method may be developed to help match the supply of this popular food fish to its enormous demand. Only yesterday we discovered a new freshwater shrimp on the market. It was shipped here from Bangladesh.

If you have the time and patience and are adventurous, you can catch shrimps yourself—that is, if you find yourself in the right location at the right time. All you need is to be in Southern Florida or the Bahamas under a good moon with a flashlight and a long-handled net. From a small boat or from a dock you can, if all conditions are right, attract shrimps to the surface with your light and dip them out with your net.

How to Buy

Shrimps are sold in almost every form imaginable—fresh and frozen, peeled and unpeeled, cooked and raw. They are sold dried, canned and smoked. Fresh or frozen shrimps are sold by the pound, but because they vary so in size the count is also important. Thus you might find them packaged at 5, 10, 20, 30, 40, up to 150 (for example) to the pound. It is important to remember that shrimps in the shell weigh twice as much as dressed shrimps. Unlike the practice in European countries of marketing the whole shrimp, custom in America dictates that it be sold with the head and, often, tail removed.

A word of caution or explanation: sometimes large shrimps are marketed as "prawns" or "scampi." These two species are actually lobsterettes, sub-members of the lobster family. But if you can't tell the difference, why worry?

Although a slight degree of iodine odor may be expected in shrimps, fresh shrimps should smell fresh and the flesh should be firm and clear.

How to Prepare

Many shrimps are sold shelled and deveined, some even breaded. To clean fresh shrimps-in-shell, drop them into salted boiling water for 5 minutes, cool, then peel off the shells and remove the black vein. Or shrimps can be peeled before cooking; use a sharp knife or a special tool made for this purpose. Shrimps that have been steamed before freezing (the pink ones), once defrosted, need almost no cooking.

How to Store

Fresh shrimps, with or without the shells, are perishable and must be kept on ice and used within 4 or 5 days of purchasing. Fresh peeled shrimps, if stored in a sealed container, may be kept in the refrigerator for a week or more. Frozen shrimps will last upward of a month if kept in the freezer, but should be used very soon once defrosted. Refreezing thawed shrimps reduces their flavor.

SHRIMP COCKTAIL SUPREME

24 medium-size shrimps, peeled, cooked and chilled	1 lemon, quartered 1½ cups Supreme Cocktail Sauce (see Index)

Arrange the shrimps around the edges of 4 salad plates or saucers, 6 on each. Place a dollop of cocktail sauce in the middle and a wedge of lemon on the side.

4 servings

This recipe may be used also for oysters, clams or lobsters.

SHRIMP SPREAD OR DIP

1 cup finely chopped peeled
   cooked shrimps
4 hard-cooked egg yolks,
   crumbled
1 tablespoon melted butter

½ teaspoon salt
few grains of cayenne
1 teaspoon dry mustard
sweet or sour cream

Blend all the ingredients, controlling the consistency with the amount of cream used—thick for a spread, thin for a dip.

about 2 cups

SHRIMP BALLS

2 cups flour
2 tablespoons baking powder
½ teaspoon curry powder
½ teaspoon salt
1 egg, beaten

½ pound peeled cooked
   shrimps, finely chopped
light cream
cooking oil

Mix together the flour, baking powder, curry powder and salt. Blend in the beaten egg, then add chopped shrimps. Stir in enough cream to moisten.

Heat oil in a large skillet to 350°F. on a frying thermometer.

Form mixture into bite-size balls and cook in hot oil until golden. Drain. Serve on toothpicks with your favorite sauce (see Index) for dipping.

6 servings

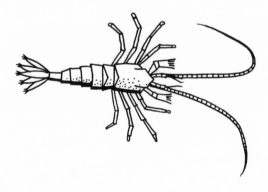

SHRIMP CHOWDER

¼ pound salt pork, diced
2 tablespoons flour
pinch of cayenne
1 teaspoon salt
3 cups milk
1 cup light cream

2 tablespoons butter
3 raw potatoes, peeled and
 diced
1 pound peeled raw shrimps,
 cut up

Sauté the pork in a large pot. Blend in the flour and seasonings. Cook for 2 minutes.

Add the milk, cream, butter and potatoes. Cook for 10 minutes, or until chowder is thickened and smooth.

Add the shrimps and simmer for 10 minutes longer.

4 servings

SHRIMP BISQUE

4 tablespoons butter
1 celery rib, chopped
2 large mushrooms, chopped
½ onion, chopped
½ carrot, chopped
pinch of dried marjoram
few grains of grated mace
½ teaspoon salt
½ teaspoon freshly ground
 pepper

1 can (10 ounces)
 concentrated chicken
 broth
1 cup water
1 cup finely chopped peeled
 cooked shrimps
1 cup heavy cream
2 teaspoons dry sherry wine

Put the butter, celery, mushrooms, onion, carrot and seasonings into a large pot and cook slowly for 10 minutes.

Add the chicken broth and water and cook for 5 minutes longer.

Put the mixture through a sieve and return to the pot.

Add the shrimps, simmer for 1 minute, and check seasonings. Stir in the cream and sherry. Do not boil.

6 servings

This recipe may be used also for lobster or crab meat.

TEMPURA-STYLE SHRIMPS

1 egg, beaten
1 cup water
1 cup flour
dash of soy sauce
oil for deep-frying

extra flour
2 dozen medium to large
  peeled raw shrimps, with
  tails left on

Make a batter of medium thickness by blending the egg, water, flour and soy sauce.

Preheat oil in a wok or frying pan to 375°F.

Dip shrimps into flour, then into batter, and put in a frying basket. Fry in deep fat until golden.

6 to 8 servings as an appetizer, 4 as an entrée

This recipe may be used also for crayfishes.

CAJUN SHRIMP GUMBO FILÉ

1 tablespoon lard
2 tablespoons flour
4 spring onions (scallions),
  chopped
½ teaspoon dried thyme
1 bay leaf
1 teaspoon salt
½ teaspoon pepper

few dashes of Tabasco
2 quarts hot water
1 cup Fish Stock (see Index)
  or clam broth
1½ pounds peeled raw
  shrimps
2 teaspoons chopped parsley
1 tablespoon filé

Heat the lard in a 3-quart pot; add the flour and brown it.

Add spring onions and seasonings and simmer for 5 minutes.

Pour in the hot water and stock. Cover and simmer over low heat for 20 minutes.

Add shrimps and parsley. Cook for 10 minutes.

Remove from heat, drop in the filé, and stir vigorously. Serve with rice.

6 servings

Note: Filé is dried young sassafras leaves, powdered, used as a flavoring and thickening agent. It is available in specialty stores and in most supermarkets. Add at the end of cooking, and do not cook again lest filé become "stringy."

NEW ORLEANS SHRIMP GUMBO

4 slices of bacon
2 tablespoons butter
2 cups sliced okra, fresh or
   canned
1 onion, chopped
1 garlic clove, crushed
1 green pepper, chopped
1 celery rib, chopped

2 tomatoes, peeled and
   chopped
pinch of dried thyme
1 quart hot water
1 teaspoon salt
½ teaspoon pepper
1 pound peeled raw shrimps

Fry the bacon until crisp; crumble and set aside.

Add the butter to the bacon fat, then add the okra, onion, garlic, green pepper and celery. Sauté for 10 minutes (less for canned okra).

Add tomatoes, thyme, hot water, seasonings and shrimps. Cover and simmer for 10 minutes longer.

Check seasonings. Serve garnished with the bacon bits.

6 servings

This recipe may be used also for crab meat.

TANGY STEAMED SHRIMPS

1 celery rib
1 bay leaf
½ garlic clove, chopped
½ teaspoon salt
½ teaspoon freshly ground
   pepper

½ cup dry white wine
½ cup water
1½ pounds raw shrimps in
   shells
melted butter

Put celery and seasonings, wine and water in a saucepan. Cover and simmer gently for 10 minutes.

Add the shrimps, cover, and simmer for 5 minutes longer. Pour off the court bouillon and save for use in other shrimp recipes.

Serve the shrimps in the shells with melted butter for dipping.

4 servings

SHRIMP PILAU

4 slices of bacon, quartered
1 onion, chopped
2 cups canned tomatoes
1 cup uncooked rice

1½ pounds peeled cooked shrimps, coarsely chopped
1 teaspoon salt
½ teaspoon pepper

Cook the bacon until crisp; remove and reserve bacon; leave fat in the pan.

Brown the onion in the bacon fat. Add the tomatoes and simmer for 5 minutes.

Transfer the mixture to the top section of a double boiler. Add the rice, and steam over boiling water for about 40 minutes, or until rice is done.

Preheat oven to 350°F.

Transfer the mixture to a baking dish; add the reserved bacon, the shrimps and seasonings. Bake for about 15 minutes, or until rather solid in texture.

4 servings

This recipe may be used also for crayfishes.

SHRIMPS IN BEER

2 pounds fresh shrimps in the shell
3 cups beer
1 garlic clove, chopped
1 teaspoon salt
½ teaspoon dried thyme

1 teaspoon celery seed
1 tablespoon minced parsley
few dashes of Tabasco
2 teaspoons lemon juice
melted butter

Mix together all the ingredients except the butter. Bring to a boil, then simmer for about 4 minutes, or until shrimps are pink. Drain.

Serve shrimps in a napkin, with melted butter on the side.

4 servings

LOUISIANA SHRIMP STEW

4 tablespoons butter
2 tablespoons flour
2 onions, chopped
1 green pepper, chopped
2 tomatoes, peeled and
   seeded
2 teaspoons chopped parsley

½ teaspoon salt
¼ teaspoon white pepper
pinch of cayenne
dash of Worcestershire
   sauce
1½ pounds peeled raw
   shrimps
2 teaspoons snipped fresh dill

Melt the butter in a saucepan, stir in the flour, then add the onions, green pepper, tomatoes and seasonings. Simmer for 5 minutes, or until vegetables are tender.

Add the shrimps, stir, cover, and cook for 10 minutes longer. Serve garnished with fresh dill.

4 servings

CHARLESTON SHRIMP "PIE"

3 slices of bread
1 cup milk
1 pound cooked peeled
   shrimps
2 tablespoons melted butter
½ teaspoon salt

¼ teaspoon pepper
1 teaspoon Worcestershire
   sauce
dash of Tabasco
2 tablespoons sherry wine

Preheat oven to 375°F.

Soak the bread in the milk and mash with a fork.

Add the shrimps, butter, seasonings and sherry; mix well. Turn into a well-buttered 9-inch pie plate.

Bake in the oven for 20 minutes.

4 servings

SHRIMP CASSEROLE WITH NOODLES

1½ cups cooked peeled
    shrimps
2 cups cooked noodles
3 hard-cooked eggs,
    quartered
1 onion, thinly sliced
1 cup sliced mushrooms
2 tablespoons butter

2 tablespoons flour
1 teaspoon salt
½ teaspoon pepper
½ teaspoon celery salt
1½ cups milk
bread crumbs
butter

Preheat oven to 375°F.

Put the shrimps, noodles, eggs, onion and mushrooms in a 2-quart casserole.

Melt the butter; stir in the flour and seasonings, then pour in the milk. Cook, stirring, until sauce is smooth and thickened. Add sauce to the casserole.

Sprinkle with bread crumbs and dot with butter. Bake for about 20 minutes, or until crumbs are brown. Serve from the casserole.

4 to 6 servings

SHRIMPS AU GRATIN

4 tablespoons butter
4 tablespoons flour
1 cup clam broth or Fish
    Stock (see Index)
1 cup cream
2 tablespoons sherry wine

1½ pounds peeled cooked
    shrimps
1 cup grated cheese
½ teaspoon salt
pinch of pepper

Preheat oven to 375°F.

Melt the butter in a saucepan, stir in the flour, and cook for 1 minute.

Mix together the broth and cream, and bring to a boil. Add to the roux, stirring until smooth and thickened.

Add the sherry, shrimps, half of the cheese and the seasonings. Place in a shallow 6-cup baking dish, and sprinkle with remaining cheese. Bake in the oven until browned.

4 to 6 servings

BAKED STUFFED SHRIMPS

8 large shrimps, peeled and
   cooked
2 cups soft bread crumbs
4 tablespoons melted butter
2 tablespoons mayonnaise
1 teaspoon dry mustard

2 tablespoons minced onion
1 garlic clove, minced
1 teaspoon salt
½ teaspoon pepper
few grains of cayenne

Preheat oven to 400°F.

Split the shrimps nearly through and open up butterfly style.

Mix remaining ingredients together and pile onto the shrimps. Place on a shallow baking pan and bake for 20 minutes, or until golden.

4 servings

SHRIMP CURRY

4 tablespoons butter
2 onions, chopped
1 garlic clove, crushed
2 cups coconut milk
2 tomatoes, peeled and
   chopped
½ cup chopped celery
1 tablespoon shredded
   coconut

1 tablespoon curry powder
   (more if you like it hot)
1 teaspoon sugar
1 tablespoon flour
½ teaspoon salt
½ teaspoon pepper
pinch of ground ginger
1½ pounds peeled cooked
   shrimps

Melt the butter in a saucepan. Sauté onions and garlic in the butter for 2 minutes. Add the coconut milk, tomatoes, celery and coconut. Bring to a boil.

Blend together the curry powder, sugar, flour, salt, pepper and ginger. Stir into the boiling mixture.

Reduce heat, cover, and simmer for about 30 minutes. Add the shrimps and cook for 5 minutes longer.

Serve on rice.

4 servings

SHRIMPS MARINIÈRE

1½ pounds peeled raw
    shrimps
2 shallots, minced, or ½ cup
    minced spring onions
    (scallions)
2 cups dry white wine
1 cup Fish Stock (see Index)
    or clam broth
2 tablespoons butter

2 tablespoons flour
1 teaspoon salt
1 tablespoon lemon juice
2 egg yolks, beaten with ½
    cup heavy cream
toast
1 tablespoon minced parsley

Simmer the shrimps and shallots in the wine and stock for 15 minutes.

Melt butter in a small skillet; stir in flour, salt and 1 cup of the shrimp liquid. (If clam broth is used omit salt.) Cook-stir until mixture thickens.

Add this sauce to the shrimps and cook over low heat for 10 minutes.

Add the lemon juice, then the egg-yolk and cream mixture, stirring constantly. Do not boil.

Serve on toast, garnished with parsley.

4 to 6 servings

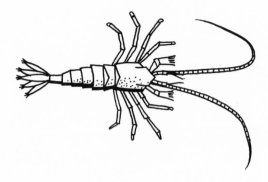

SHRIMPS À LA NEWBURG

2 tablespoons butter
1 tablespoon flour
½ teaspoon salt
½ teaspoon white pepper
¼ teaspoon dry mustard
dash of Tabasco
few grains of cayenne

1½ cups light cream
2 egg yolks, beaten
1½ pounds peeled cooked
   shrimps, coarsely cut up
4 tablespoons sherry wine
toast
minced parsley

Melt butter in the top section of a double boiler over simmering water; stir in the flour, then the seasonings. Cook for 3 minutes, stirring.

Stir in the cream until well blended. Remove from heat, and cool.

Pour the sauce over the beaten egg yolks. Add shrimps, then the sherry. Return to the double boiler and reheat.

Serve on toast, garnished with parsley.

4 to 6 servings

SCALLOPED SHRIMPS

¾ cup dry bread crumbs
½ teaspoon paprika
⅛ teaspoon grated nutmeg
½ teaspoon salt
1½ pounds peeled raw
   shrimps

2 celery ribs, chopped
1 tablespoon minced parsley
1 cup light cream
½ cup sherry wine
½ cup melted butter

Preheat oven to 350°F.

Mix together the bread crumbs, paprika, nutmeg and salt.

Place a layer of shrimps in a buttered 6-cup casserole and cover with a layer of the seasoned bread crumbs. Add a layer of celery and parsley. Repeat until all ingredients are used up, saving some of the crumbs for the top.

Pour cream and sherry over the shrimps. Sift the remaining bread crumbs over the top and sprinkle on the melted butter. Bake in the oven for 20 minutes.

4 servings

MEXICAN PANBROILED SHRIMPS

24 large fresh shrimps, peeled
    and deveined but with
    tails left on
½ cup lime juice
½ cup coconut oil or olive oil
4 garlic cloves, chopped

2 or 3 green chiles, peeled
    and chopped, or ½
    teaspoon cayenne
1 teaspoon salt
3 tablespoons butter
minced parsley

Marinate the shrimps overnight in the lime juice, oil, garlic, chiles
and salt, stirring from time to time.

Remove shrimps from the marinade and panbroil in butter for 5
minutes on each side. Serve garnished with parsley.

4 servings

SAUTÉED SHRIMPS, MUSTARD SAUCE

2 pounds peeled fresh
    shrimps
salt
2 tablespoons butter
2 tablespoons dry mustard

1 teaspoon flour
1 teaspoon sugar
½ cup heavy cream
1 egg yolk
½ cup warm vinegar

Salt the shrimps and sauté them in butter for 5 minutes on each
side. Skewer with food picks and keep warm.

Put into the top part of a double boiler, over steaming water, the
mustard, flour, ¼ teaspoon salt, sugar and cream. Heat, stirring,
for 5 minutes. Beat in the egg yolk and then the vinegar. Serve as
a dip for the shrimps.

4 to 6 servings

This recipe may be used also for crayfishes.

BUTTERFLY SHRIMPS

2 pounds peeled large raw
    shrimps, with tails left on
flour
2 eggs, beaten

cracker crumbs
oil for deep-frying
salt and pepper

Preheat oil in a saucepan or wok to 375°F.

Cut the shrimps lengthwise almost into halves and flatten out.

Dip shrimps into flour, then into beaten eggs. Dust with cracker crumbs. Place a few at a time in a frying basket and fry until golden.

Season to taste. Serve with Tartar Sauce (see Index) or any other sauce of your choice.

4 to 6 servings

This recipe may be used also for small spiny lobsters or crayfishes.

SHRIMP FRITTERS

2 cups flour	1 cup milk
1 tablespoon baking powder	1½ pounds peeled raw
½ teaspoon salt	shrimps, finely chopped
2 eggs, beaten	or pounded in a mortar
	3 cups cooking oil

Sift together flour, baking powder and salt. Beat in the eggs, then the milk, to form a batter. Stir chopped shrimps into the batter.

Heat oil in a large skillet to 375°F. on a frying thermometer.

Drop batter by the spoonful into hot oil and cook for 3 minutes, or until fritters are golden. Remove and drain.

Serve with your favorite sauce (see Index).

4 servings

This recipe may be used also for crab meat.

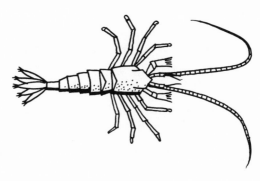

BEER-FRIED SHRIMPS

1½ pounds peeled raw
    shrimps
½ teaspoon Worcestershire
    sauce
½ cup flour
pinch of salt
1 teaspoon melted butter

1 egg, beaten
½ cup beer
fat for deep-frying
4 tablespoons minced
    cranberries mixed with 4
    tablespoons fresh
    horseradish

Brush the shrimps well with Worcestershire sauce.

Sift the flour and salt together; stir in the butter, egg and beer until mixture is smooth.

Heat fat to 365°F. on a frying thermometer.

Dip the shrimps, a few at a time, into the batter. Fry in deep fat for 3 to 5 minutes, or until golden. Serve with horseradish-cranberry sauce.

4 servings

SHRIMP PATTIES

2 cups peeled cooked shrimps
4 slices of not-too-fresh bread,
    crusts removed

¼ cup melted butter
    containing ½ teaspoon
    each of grated mace, salt
    and pepper
2 cups Béchamel Sauce (see
    Index)

Preheat oven to 275°F.

Pound the shrimps in a mortar, or run them through a meat grinder or process them in a blender.

Soak the bread in water, squeeze dry, and crumble into the shrimps.

Mix in the savory butter. Shape the mixture into small cakes. Place in a buttered pan and bake for 15 minutes, or until brown.

Serve with béchamel sauce.

4 servings

SOUTHERN FRIED SHRIMPS

2 pounds peeled raw shrimps, with tails intact
1 cup cracker crumbs
½ cup flour

1 teaspoon curry powder
½ teaspoon salt
3 cups cooking oil
2 eggs, beaten

Split shrimps open lengthwise and flatten out.

Mix together cracker crumbs, flour, curry powder and salt.

Heat oil in a large skillet to 350°F. on a frying thermometer.

Dip shrimps into beaten eggs and roll in flour mixture. Fry in hot oil for 3 minutes, or until golden. Remove and drain.

Serve with your favorite sauce (see Index).

4 servings

SHRIMPS IN ASPIC

½ cup warm water
2 envelopes unflavored gelatin
1 cup Fish Stock (see Index) or clam broth

2 cups coarsely chopped cooked shrimps
1 cup chopped celery
lettuce

Dissolve the gelatin in the warm water; stir in the stock; pour half of this mixture into a wet 1-quart mold; chill until slightly firm.

Combine shrimps and celery and arrange on top of the set gelatin. Cover with remaining (still liquid) gelatin. Cover and chill for 3 to 4 hours, or until firm.

Dip the mold into hot water and turn out the aspic onto a bed of chilled lettuce.

4 servings

This recipe may be used also with cooked crab meat, lobster meat or scallops.

TEXAS SHRIMP ENCHILADAS

SAUCE

6 tablespoons chili powder
1½ garlic cloves, minced
1 teaspoon ground cuminseed
4 cups beef broth

2 tablespoons cornstarch
   mixed with 1 tablespoon
   water

Simmer the chili powder, garlic and cuminseed in the broth for 2 minutes. Add the cornstarch and cook for 2 minutes longer. Reserve and keep hot.

FILLING

1 onion, chopped
1 garlic clove, minced
2 tablespoons cooking oil
2 cups finely chopped cooked shrimps
2 cups grated Monterey Jack or mild Cheddar cheese

12 tortillas
oil

Sauté the onion and garlic in the oil; stir in the shrimps, ½ cup of the reserved sauce, and half of the cheese. Cook for 2 minutes. Set aside and keep hot.

Preheat oven to 400°F.

Fry tortillas, one at a time, in oil, then dip into the sauce. Spoon some filling onto each tortilla. Roll tortillas tightly.

Place tortillas side by side in a shallow baking pan. Sprinkle with the remaining cheese. Bake in the oven for 10 minutes. Spoon hot sauce over all.

4 servings

Part Two

BIVALVE
MOLLUSKS

CLAMS
MUSSELS
OYSTERS
SCALLOPS

CLAMS

Clams were a favorite food of Americans long before the arrival of the Pilgrims, the Virginia colonists and the Spanish conquistadors. Those early Americans, the Indians, also used the shells, which they formed into beads and strung into necklaces or belts, as a medium of exchange—wampum.

Although wampum has become extinct almost as much as the buffalo (nickel, that is), the clam itself has survived and is prized as food from coast to coast.

Clams, bivalve mollusks, are found along the sandy shores of the United States, East, West and South. They thrive prolifically on the deepwater Continental Shelf of the Atlantic Coast. The variety of clam species seems almost endless: Beach Clam, Surf Clam, Sea Clam, Skimmer; Bean Clam, Coquina, Butter Clam and Geoduck; Quahaug, Cherrystone, Little Neck and Chowder; Razor Clam, Softshell, Steamer and Ipswich; Sunray, Giant Callista, Butter Clam, Bar Clam and Pismo. And then there is the Cockle, popular in England (grown by Mistress Mary and sold on the streets of Dublin "alive, alive-oh"). Confusing? Yes, especially when each species, depending upon its milieu, can have more than one name.

By far the most popular of all clams is the Quahaug (sometimes spelled Quahog). The smallest of these is the Little Neck (named for the bay on Long Island). Next largest is the Cherrystone (originally from Cherrystone Creek in Virginia). The largest, of course is the Chowder Clam, too tough except for use in chowders.

Quahaugs are found in shallow waters all up and down the East Coast, and to a slight degree on the Pacific Coast. They are harvested commercially by raking or dredging. You can gather them yourself by "toeing" them—by wading in shallow water until your toes make contact.

Almost as popular is the Maninose or Soft Clam, usually called a Steamer or Ipswich (after the river in Massachusetts). This clam buries itself in the sand and can be dug out at high tide as it

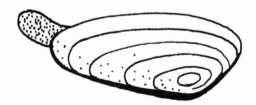

betrays its hiding place by squirting water from its "neck" or siphon. More plentiful in New England waters, this delicate and sweet-tasting clam is eaten only after cooking—steaming or frying.

The Razor Clam (it resembles the old-fashioned straight razor, and its shell often seems as sharp) is found on both coasts. But the Razor Clam has a very delicate shell, is quick acting, and is therefore not easy to come by. Upon discovery, it rapidly digs deep into the sand, and efforts to retrieve it most often result in a crushed shell. Sportsmen have devised various ways of outwitting the elusive little creature. Serious diggers in the State of

Washington often employ a 5-inch-round metal tube which they press down into the sand surrounding the clam. By closing off the top end they create a suction and pull the clam to the surface. Razor Clams may not be worth all that effort since the meat, judged by some standards, is far from tender. Digging Razor

Clams commercially has never proved successful, due not only to the fragility of the shell but also to its open-endedness which makes it impossible for the clam to retain its vital juices when removed from the sea.

California's largest clams, the Pismo and Geoduck (pronounced gooey-duck), once plentiful along the coast from San Francisco to Baja California, have become so rare as to be almost extinct. The latter, which grows to almost 7 inches across the shell and has a "neck" or siphon up to a yard long, once provided great sport at full-moon low tides. The tough meat was extracted, sliced, and consumed like abalone.

There is a Sunray Clam, also known as a Callista, in the southern waters of Florida and South Carolina.

Cockles, especially prized in Europe, are found on the Pacific Coast, and a species too small to be considered appears along the Atlantic.

Surf Clams (Bar Clams, Skimmers), the largest of the Quahaugs, are dredged commercially from deep waters from New Jersey north to Canada in vast quantities. The tough meat is ground to make chowder, stuffed clams and sauces.

Bean Clams of the Pacific (Coquinas on Florida's West Coast) are the smallest of all useful clams. Measuring about ¾ inch long, they are too small for any purpose other than soup-making.

How to Buy

Clams are found in the market in a number of forms: in the shell and shucked; canned whole, canned minced, and smoked. Clam juice and broth are bottled. Clams in the shell are sold by the dozen or by the pound. Be sure they are live, with shells tightly closed. Shucked clams are sold by the pint or quart; they should be fresh, plump and in clear liquid. Clams are also sold fresh frozen. Several varieties of clams are canned whole or minced, and then heat processed.

How to Prepare

To shuck hardshell clams:

a. Scrub shells well under running cold water.
b. Hold clam in palm of hand with hinge toward thumb.
c. Insert clam knife between shells; run knife around clam and twist.
d. Cut muscle holding top shell and twist off top shell.
e. Run knife under clam, cutting bottom muscle.

(If you intend to cook clams, you can open them by steaming. This goes for soft clams, as well.)

Soft clams can be desanded by soaking for a few hours in cold salted water containing a handful of cornmeal. They thus purge themselves of the sand and at the same time plump by osmosis.

How to Store

Hard clams constrict the adductor muscles when chilled and tighten the two valves or shells, retaining their vital fluids. Thus they will survive for a month at least if kept well refrigerated. Soft clams possess a protruding neck that prevents tight closure and they depend upon a membrane for juice retention. If kept under constant refrigeration they will live for a week or longer. Razor clams and a few other species are open-ended and therefore short-lived once removed from their habitat. Any open-shelled mollusk that does not clam up when tapped is to be strictly avoided.

CLAM SPREAD OR DIP

8 ounces cream cheese
1 tablespoon Worcestershire
    sauce
½ garlic clove, minced

2 tablespoons dry white wine
    or dry vermouth
1 tablespoon clam juice
1 can (8 ounces) minced clams

Mix all the ingredients together and serve on toast squares.

For clam dip, thin down to desired consistency with additional clam broth.

about 2 cups

CLAMS ORÉGANATO

24 large Little Neck clams or
    small Cherrystones
2 tablespoons butter
1 medium-size onion,
    chopped
¼ cup chopped green pepper
½ garlic clove, minced

1 egg, beaten
2 cups dry bread crumbs
¼ teaspoon dried basil
1 teaspoon dried orégano
few drops of Worcestershire
few grains of cayenne
olive oil

Preheat oven to 400°F.

Scrub and shuck the clams, reserving the bottom shells. Chop the meat and reserve.

Melt the butter and sauté the onion, green pepper and garlic until browned.

Mix together the beaten egg, bread crumbs, basil, half of the orégano, the Worcestershire and cayenne.

Blend in the chopped clams and the onion mixture. Pile into the clam shells, brush with olive oil, and sprinkle with remaining orégano. Bake in the oven until golden. Serve as a first course.

6 to 8 servings

CLAMS CASINO

6 slices of bacon
½ cup minced shallots or
    spring onions (scallions)
¼ cup minced green pepper
¼ cup minced celery
few drops of Worcestershire
    sauce

few drops of Tabasco
24 large Little Necks or small
    Cherrystone clams on the
    half shell

Preheat oven to 400°F.

Cook the bacon until crisp. Drain, dry, and crumble; reserve.

To the bacon fat add the shallots, green pepper, celery, Worcestershire and Tabasco. Cook for a minute or two.

Spoon this sauce over the half-shell clams, and top with the crumbled bacon. Bake in the oven for 5 minutes, or until sauce bubbles.

8 servings as an appetizer, 4 as an entrée

This recipe may be used also for oysters.

STEAMED IPSWICHES

A clam steamer is a double-compartmented cooker; the top part, where the clams go, is perforated. The bottom compartment, usually with a spigot for running off broth, contains a little water which, when heated, steams up into the compartment, to cook the clams. The process is simple and can be accomplished with makeshift utensils such as a pot of suitable size, a colander and a lid to hold in the steam.

To eat soft clams, remove them from the shells and dip them into broth to remove any sand that may be present; then dip clams into melted butter. When serving, allow at least a dozen per person.

This recipe may be used also for mussels.

CLAM BROTH

Clam broth can be used as a soup or to flavor other seafood dishes; or you can chill it, mix with tomato juice or chili sauce, and serve as a cocktail.

Put 2 dozen or more well-scrubbed soft clams (or any other kind) into a pot with 2 cups water. Cover tightly and steam for 30 minutes. Strain. The less water used the more concentrated the broth.

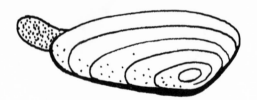

MANHATTAN CLAM CHOWDER

¼ pound salt pork, diced
1 onion, chopped
1 cup cubed raw potatoes
1 cup chopped green pepper
2 cups water
2 cups canned tomatoes

1 pint shucked chowder
    clams, finely chopped
¼ teaspoon dried thyme
½ teaspoon salt
½ teaspoon pepper

Put the diced pork into a deep saucepan and cook until fat melts.

Add the onion, potatoes and green pepper, and simmer for 15 minutes. Add the water and tomatoes.

Add the chopped clams. Season with thyme, salt and pepper. Simmer for 3 minutes.

4 servings

NEW ENGLAND CLAM CHOWDER

¼ pound salt pork, diced
4 medium-size onions,
    chopped
1 cup clam broth
2 cups diced raw potatoes
1 quart milk
3 cups ground or chopped
    quahaugs

1 teaspoon salt
1 teaspoon pepper
½ cup flour mixed with 2
    tablespoons melted butter
thyme

Brown the salt pork in a large pot or kettle until crisp and nutty. Add the onions and sauté until golden.

Add the clam broth, potatoes, milk, quahaugs, seasonings and butter-flour mixture. Cook without boiling for 15 minutes, or until potatoes are softened.

Serve in soup bowls with crackers and a shaker of dried thyme on the table.

4 to 6 servings

CHARLESTON CHOWDER

3 dozen Cherrystones, or 2
  dozen chowder clams
4 slices of bacon, chopped
2 medium-size onions,
  chopped
2½ cups diced raw potatoes

3 cups additional clam broth
4 cups milk
salt and pepper
4 tablespoons butter
2 tablespoons flour

Scrub the clams. Steam them open; strain and reserve the broth. Grind the clams.

Sauté the bacon and onions until crisp and golden.

Put the clams, bacon, onions and diced potatoes into a kettle with just enough water to cover and cook until potatoes are done.

Add the reserved broth, the extra broth and milk. Season as desired. Thicken with *beurre manié* made by mixing the butter and flour.

8 to 10 servings

CLAM BELLY SOUP

We discovered this superb soup at Gage & Tollner, a gas-light restaurant that has been on Fulton Street in Brooklyn since 1879.

2 dozen soft clams, scrubbed
2 cups light cream
2 tablespoons melted butter
pinch of grated mace or
  nutmeg

pinch of salt
1 teaspoon sherry wine

Steam the clams in a little water until the shells open.

Remove the soft round bellies, reserving the necks and other parts for another recipe. Strain the broth.

Combine the cream, butter and seasonings, and mix in enough of the strained broth to give the desired consistency.

Add the reserved clam bellies and the sherry. Heat gently and serve in cups.

2 servings

CLAM BISQUE

clams: 6 chowders, 12
    Cherrystones, or 24 Little
    Necks
1 celery rib, chopped
1 slice of onion, chopped
1 parsley sprig, chopped

½ bay leaf
¼ pound butter
¼ cup flour
pinch of cayenne
¼ teaspoon white pepper
2 cups light cream

Scrub and open the clams, reserving the juice. Chop the clams or put through a food grinder. Reserve.

Put the celery, onion, parsley, bay leaf and reserved clam juice into a saucepan, and simmer gently for 10 minutes. Strain and reserve.

Melt the butter, stir in the flour and seasonings, cook for a minute, then gradually stir in the reserved liquid and cook over low heat until the sauce is smooth and thickened.

Add the reserved clams and the cream. Heat, stirring, but do not boil.

4 servings

CLAM STEW AU NATUREL

1 tablespoon butter
1 teaspoon Worcestershire
    sauce
1 teaspoon paprika

½ teaspoon celery salt
1 dozen Cherrystone clams in
    their juices

Put all the ingredients in a heavy saucepan and bring to a quick boil. Reduce the heat and simmer for 1 or 2 minutes. Serve promptly.

2 servings

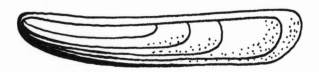

GRAND CENTRAL CLAM PAN ROAST

2 tablespoons butter
1 teaspoon Worcestershire
    sauce
1 teaspoon paprika
1 dozen Cherrystones
    (chopped, if desired)

½ cup clam juice
2 tablespoons chili sauce
1 cup cream
1 teaspoon lemon juice
dry toast (optional)

Put the butter, Worcestershire, paprika and clams into the top section of a double boiler over boiling water, cook up, and let froth for ½ minute.

Stir in clam juice and chili sauce and cook for 1 minute longer.

Add the cream, then the lemon juice, and stir for ½ minute. Serve in bowls or on toast.

2 servings

This recipe may be used also for oysters.

SCALLOPED CLAMS

2 cups minced Cherrystones
    or Little Necks, with juice
1 cup cracker crumbs
1 cup milk or half-and-half

¼ cup melted butter
½ teaspoon pepper
1 egg, beaten

Mix all the ingredients together and let stand for 30 minutes.

Preheat oven to 350°F.

Transfer clam mixture to a buttered 4-cup casserole and bake for 20 minutes.

4 servings

STUFFED CHERRYSTONES

1 dozen Cherrystone clams,
    scrubbed
1 onion, minced
½ garlic clove, minced
2-inch square of salt pork
    ¼ inch thick, finely
    chopped

pinch of pepper
dash of Tabasco
dash of Worcestershire sauce
½ cup cracker crumbs
1 egg, lightly beaten

Preheat oven to 350°F.

Steam the clams open, or open by hand, but leave the shells hinged.

Drain juice into a bowl, add the quahaugs, and mince. Add the minced onion and garlic, chopped salt pork and seasonings.

Soak the cracker crumbs in a little clam juice, and squeeze out. Add moistened crumbs and the egg to the bowl.

Mix thoroughly, and stuff into the hinged shells. Close shells and tie tightly. Place in a shallow pan and bake for about 20 minutes.

4 to 6 servings

This recipe may be used also for oysters.

SOFT CLAMS FISHERMAN STYLE

4 dozen softshell clams, well
    scrubbed
1 medium-size onion,
    chopped
1 bay leaf
2 tablespoons minced parsley
pinch of dried thyme

pinch of dried dill
1 cup dry white wine
2 tablespoons butter
2 tablespoons flour
salt and pepper
French bread

Put the clams, onion, bay leaf, parsley, thyme, dill and wine into a large kettle. Cover and steam over high heat for 2 minutes or until shells open.

Remove the clams to 4 bowls and keep warm.

Strain the sauce and stir in *beurre manié* made by blending the butter and flour. Season to taste.

Pour sauce over the clams and serve with crusty French bread.

4 servings

This recipe may be used also for mussels.

NANTUCKET CLAM PIE

1 dozen Cherrystone or 2
   dozen Little Neck clams,
   shucked
2 medium-size raw potatoes,
   peeled and thinly sliced
2 medium-size onions, thinly
   sliced

2 tablespoons melted butter
1 cup light cream
½ teaspoon pepper
pastry for 1-crust deep-dish
   pie

Preheat oven to 450°F.

Chop clams; save the juice.

Put the clams, potatoes and onions in layers into a 2-quart casserole. Add the reserved juice, butter, cream and pepper.

Cover with pastry; perforate pastry with steam vents. Bake for about 30 minutes, or until crust is browned.

4 servings

This recipe may be used also for razor clams or steamers (tough necks discarded).

DEVILED CLAMS

2 tablespoons butter
1 medium-size onion, minced
½ green pepper, minced
1 celery rib, minced
1 pimiento, chopped
½ teaspoon dry mustard
½ teaspoon Worcestershire
   sauce

dash of Tabasco
½ cup dry bread crumbs
1 dozen Cherrystones with
   juice and shells
¼ cup dry white wine
minced parsley

Preheat oven to 375°F.

Melt the butter and sauté the onion, green pepper and celery for 3 minutes.

Stir in the pimiento, seasonings, bread crumbs, Cherrystones and wine. Moisten with clam juice if necessary.

Pile into clam shells, 1 clam to a shell, and bake in the oven for 20 minutes. Garnish with parsley.

4 servings

This recipe may be used also for oysters.

NEW ORLEANS CLAMS CREOLE

2 tablespoons butter
1 onion, minced
2 tablespoons flour
1 cup tomato sauce
½ cup chopped green pepper
1 teaspoon chopped parsley
¼ teaspoon thyme
few grains of cayenne
2 dozen shucked Little Neck
clams, drained
buttered toast points

Melt the butter, stir in the onion, and cook for 1 minute. Stir in the flour and cook for 1 minute longer.

Add the tomato sauce, green pepper, parsley, thyme and cayenne. Simmer, stirring, until the sauce is thickened.

Stir in the Little Necks and heat for 1 or 2 minutes (longer will toughen the clams). Serve on toast.

4 servings

This recipe may be used also for oysters.

NEW BEDFORD CLAM PATTIES

2 cups ground or chopped
Cherrystones or Little
Necks, with juice
2 eggs, well beaten
¾ cup cracker crumbs
1 teaspoon paprika
cooking oil

Mix together the clams, beaten eggs, cracker crumbs and paprika.

Drop by tablespoons onto a hot oiled griddle, and cook for about 4 minutes on each side, or until golden brown.

4 servings

FRIED IPSWICHES

1 cup flour	½ cup milk
1 teaspoon baking powder	24 softshell clams
¼ teaspoon salt	oil for deep-frying
2 eggs, beaten until fluffy	

Sift together the flour, baking powder and salt, and beat in the eggs and milk with a wire whisk.

Open the clam shells with a knife, remove the clams, and dry well with a paper towel.

Heat cooking oil to 350°F. on a frying thermometer.

Dip clams into the batter. Deep-fry in hot oil for 2 to 3 minutes, or until golden.

4 servings

This recipe may be used also for razor clams and mussels.

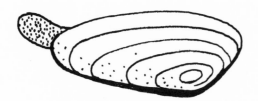

FRIED CLAMS ON THE HALF SHELL

16 Cherrystones in the shell	dash of Tabasco
2 eggs, beaten	flour
½ teaspoon salt	fat for frying
¼ teaspoon pepper	

Shuck the clams, discarding the top shells, and strain and reserve the juice. Place clams shell side up to drain. Wipe dry with paper towels.

Mix together the beaten eggs, 2 tablespoons of the juice, salt, pepper and Tabasco.

Dip the clams, shells and all, into the egg mixture, and roll in flour. Fry, shell side up, in hot fat until golden.

4 servings

QUAHAUG BEER FRITTERS

2 cups flour
1 teaspoon baking powder
2 eggs, beaten
dash of Tabasco
1 cup beer

1 pint shucked fresh
   quahaugs, minced, with
   juice
bacon fat or cooking oil

Sift together flour and baking powder. Stir in the eggs, Tabasco and beer to make a smooth batter.

Stir in the minced clams. Drop by tablespoons onto a hot greased griddle. Cook for about 6 minutes on each side, or until golden.

6 servings

FRIED GEODUCKS

oil for deep-frying
4 geoducks, cut into ¼-inch-
   thick slices (discard the
   necks or grind them for
   chowder)

½ teaspoon salt
½ teaspoon pepper
milk
1 egg, beaten
flour

Preheat oil to 370°F. on a frying thermometer.

Dry the geoduck slices well. Season them with salt and pepper, dip them into milk, then into beaten egg, then into flour.

Place slices, a few at a time, in a wire basket and deep-fry for a few minutes until golden.

4 servings

WHITE CLAM SAUCE (FOR PASTA)

¼ cup light Lucca style Italian olive oil
3 garlic cloves, finely chopped
½ cup finely chopped parsley
12 Cherrystone clams, coarsely chopped, with juice
½ teaspoon salt
¼ teaspoon pepper

Heat the oil; stir in the remaining ingredients. Remove from heat and keep hot.

Stir into 1 pound spaghetti cooked *al dente* and serve immediately.

6 servings

RED CLAM SAUCE (FOR PASTA)

¼ cup light Lucca style Italian olive oil
1 garlic clove, finely chopped
2 cups chopped tomatoes
½ teaspoon dried marjoram
½ teaspoon dried sweet basil
1 teaspoon salt
¼ teaspoon pepper
12 Cherrystone clams, coarsely chopped

Heat the oil; add the garlic and cook until golden. Add the tomatoes and seasonings and cook for 30 minutes, or until sauce is thick. Stir in the clams; do not cook further, but keep hot.

Stir into 1 pound spaghetti cooked *al dente* and serve immediately.

6 servings

MUSSELS

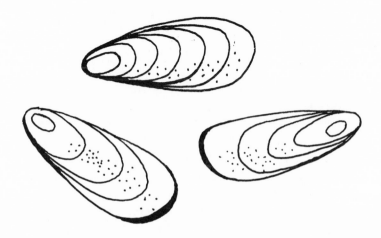

Mussels, like oysters and clams, are bivalve mollusks. Although they are found throughout the world in both fresh and marine waters, none of the freshwater and few of the seawater species are esculent. Green Mussels, Hooked Mussels, Scorched Mussels, Horse Mussels and most of the other varieties have little or no gastronomic value and will not be considered here.

The Blue Mussel is a gastronomic treat of the greatest importance. Growing in clumps or colonies on rocks, seawalls, shipwrecks, piles or any other object to which it may attach itself, the Blue Mussel is found along the Atlantic Coast as far south as the Carolinas and along the shores of California where it was recently introduced.

The Blue Mussel, so called because of its satiny dark blue shell, starts out, like the oyster, as a "spat" swimming about and looking for a home to which it may attach itself. This it does by means of

97

its "beard" of silky threads. The Blue Mussel grows quickly and reaches a length of up to 4 inches or more. The fragile oval shells, violet-tinted inside, enclose a creamy golden-white body, largely adductor muscle, deliciously tender and sweet.

In Europe—and to a lesser extent in the United States—Blue Mussels are cultivated in large quantities to satisfy the ever-growing appetites of aficionados. Ropes suspended into the sea or stakes driven into the shallow coastal waters quickly become covered by the little "spats" which develop at a rapid rate into harvestable nutritious food, rich in protein, vitamins and minerals. Mussels may well provide the cheapest nutrition available in today's market.

How to Buy

Mussels are sold by the pound, refrigerated live in the shell, usually during the fall, winter and early spring. The meat is also available cooked and frozen, and canned fresh or smoked.

How to Prepare

Mussels should be carefully picked over and the dead ones discarded. (If the mussel can move its shell, it is alive.) They must then be scrubbed well, preferably with a wire brush, to remove dirt, grass and the "beard." After cooking, discard any mussels with *unopened* shells.

How to Store

Fresh mussels will keep in the refrigerator for as long as 2 weeks, but inevitably some will be found dead. Those with open shells should be regarded with suspicion, but if the shells move when tapped, the mussel is alive.

STEAMED MUSSELS, PLAIN

3 dozen mussels, scrubbed   1 teaspoon salt
   and debearded

Pour 1 inch of water into a heavy pot, stir in the salt, and add the mussels. Cover and cook for 3 minutes, or until shells begin to open. Discard any mussels with unopened shells. Serve in bowls with the strained broth.

4 servings

SAFFRON MUSSELS ON STICKS

3 tablespoons olive oil
1 onion, chopped
2 leeks, white part only, cut
    up
2 tomatoes, cut up
½ garlic clove, chopped
pinch of dried thyme

1 bay leaf
pinch of ground saffron
1 teaspoon salt
½ teaspoon pepper
1 cup dry white wine
3 dozen mussels, scrubbed
    and debearded

Heat the oil in a saucepan and sauté the onion and leeks for 2 minutes. Add the tomatoes, garlic, seasonings and wine. Cook until liquid is reduced to about ½ cup, and strain.

Cover mussels with water and cook covered until shells open, discarding any unopened. Remove mussels from shells, put into a bowl, pour the savory sauce over them, and refrigerate.

Serve on toothpicks at cocktail time.

4 servings

This recipe may be used also for soft clams.

MUSSELS MARINIÈRE

¼ pound butter
3 tablespoons chopped
    shallots or scallions
pinch of dried thyme
¼ bay leaf
3 dozen mussels, scrubbed
    and debearded

½ teaspoon salt
½ teaspoon white pepper
1 cup dry white wine
½ cup heavy cream mixed
    with 2 egg yolks
2 teaspoons minced parsley

Melt the butter in a large saucepan and gently sauté the shallots, thyme and bay leaf for a minute or so.

Add the mussels (only those with tightly closed shells), sprinkle with salt and pepper, and pour in the wine. Cover and cook over high heat for 10 minutes, or until shells open.

Remove the mussels, still in shells, to 4 heated soup bowls. Strain the liquid, and thicken with the cream and egg-yolk mixture.

Pour the sauce over the mussels, sprinkle with minced parsley, and serve with crusty French bread.

4 to 6 servings

MUSSELS WITH BACON

3 dozen mussels, scrubbed
    and debearded
6 slices of bacon, cut into
    strips 2 inches x ½ inch

curry powder
celery seed

Preheat oven to 450°F.

Remove mussels from shells and place on bacon strips, 1 mussel per square. Roll up, fasten with toothpicks, and place in a shallow baking dish.

Season each mussel with a pinch of curry powder. Place them under the broiler for 2 minutes, or until bacon is crisp. Dip into celery seed and serve hot.

6 to 8 servings

This recipe may be used also for soft clams.

MUSSELS IN SNAIL BUTTER

½ pound sweet butter,
    softened
2 tablespoons finely chopped
    shallots
1 garlic clove, mashed
2 tablespoons finely chopped
    parsley
¼ teaspoon salt

pinch of pepper
pinch of grated nutmeg
3 dozen large mussels (4
    dozen, if small), scrubbed
    and debearded
fine bread crumbs
½ cup dry white wine

Preheat oven to 400°F.

In a mixing bowl cream the butter, shallots, garlic, parsley and seasonings.

Open the mussels as you would clams. Leave mussels in bottom shells, discarding top shells.

Arrange mussels side by side in a shallow baking pan. Cover each one with some of the snail butter. Sprinkle with bread crumbs and pour in the wine.

Bake in the oven for 8 minutes.

4 to 6 servings

MAINE BAKED MUSSELS WITH
BACON AND CHEESE

3 dozen large mussels,
　　scrubbed and debearded
2 teaspoons salt
½ teaspoon pepper

½ cup minced onion
9 slices of bacon, cut into
　　quarters
½ cup grated American
　　cheese

Preheat oven to 300°F.

Open the mussels as you would clams. Leave mussels in bottom shells, discarding top shells.

Arrange mussels side by side in a shallow baking pan. Sprinkle with salt, pepper and minced onion.

Lay bacon pieces on top, and sprinkle with cheese. Bake in the oven until bacon is crisp.

8 servings as appetizer, 4 as entrée

This recipe may be used also for soft clams.

MUSSEL VELOUTÉ

3 dozen mussels, scrubbed
　　and debearded
½ cup dry white wine
1 tablespoon chopped parsley
pinch of dried thyme
few grains of cayenne
¼ pound butter
4 shallots or spring onions
　　(scallions), chopped

1 garlic clove, chopped
2 cups hot water
1 cup hot milk
2 egg yolks, beaten
½ cup cream
1 teaspoon lemon juice
1 teaspoon salt
½ teaspoon pepper

Put the mussels in a pot with the wine, parsley, thyme and cayenne. Cook until shells open; discard any that do not open. Strain the broth and reserve. Remove mussels from shells and reserve.

Melt the butter; sauté shallots and garlic in butter until golden. Add the water, reserved broth and then the milk. Simmer for 10 minutes.

Mix together egg yolks, cream and lemon juice; stir in a little of the hot sauce, and return mixture to the pot. Add the mussels and check seasonings.

4 servings

BILLI-BI

3 dozen mussels, scrubbed
  and debearded
2 tablespoons butter
½ garlic clove, minced
2 tablespoons flour
½ teaspoon salt
¼ teaspoon pepper

few grains of cayenne
½ teaspoon paprika
½ teaspoon ground celery
  seed
1 cup dry white wine
1 cup heavy cream

Place mussels in a heavy pot with 1 cup water. Cover and cook for 5 minutes, or until shells begin to open. Remove mussels and reserve for another recipe. Strain the broth through several thicknesses of muslin.

Melt the butter; stir in the garlic, flour and seasonings. Add the reserved broth and the wine. Bring to a boil, then add the cream. Heat and serve.

4 servings

TOMATO MUSSEL BISQUE

3 dozen mussels, scrubbed
  and debearded
4 tablespoons butter
2 tablespoons flour
1 small onion, finely chopped
2 cups milk

1 can (16 ounces) tomatoes,
  drained and chopped
1 teaspoon salt
½ teaspoon freshly ground
  pepper

Place mussels in a large pot, cover with water, and steam until shells open. Remove mussels from shells and chop finely. Reserve. Strain the broth.

In a heavy saucepan melt the butter; stir in the flour and onion. Cook but do not brown. Gradually stir in the milk; then 2 cups of the reserved broth. Heat, but do not boil, to make a smooth thickened sauce.

Stir in the tomatoes, the seasonings and the reserved mussels. Heat again and serve.

4 servings

MUSSELS WITH CREAM SAUCE

3 dozen mussels, scrubbed
    and debearded
salt
2 tablespoons butter

3 tablespoons flour
1 cup heavy cream
¼ teaspoon pepper

Put the mussels in a heavy pot with about 1 cup water and 1 teaspoon salt. Cover and cook for 3 minutes, or until shells open. Discard mussels with unopened shells. Strain and reserve the broth. Remove and discard top shells.

Melt the butter, stir in the flour, and cook for a few minutes. Stir in enough of the broth to make a smooth, thick sauce. Stir in the cream; add ½ teaspoon salt and the pepper.

Arrange the mussels on a heated platter and spoon some of the sauce into each one.

4 servings

CURRIED MUSSELS

¼ pound butter
3 tablespoons chopped
    shallots or green onions
    (scallions)
pinch of dried thyme
3 dozen large mussels,
    scrubbed and debearded

½ teaspoon salt
½ teaspoon finely ground
    pepper
1 cup dry white wine
2 teaspoons curry powder
2 tablespoons Béchamel Sauce
    (see Index)

Melt the butter in a large saucepan and sauté the shallots and thyme for 2 minutes.

Add the mussels and seasoning and pour in the wine. Cover and cook for 5 minutes, or until shells open, discarding any with unopened shells.

Remove the mussels, still in shells, to a heated tureen. Strain the liquid.

Stir curry powder and béchamel sauce into the liquid. Simmer for 5 minutes, and pour over the mussels.

4 servings

MUSSELS, NEWPORT STYLE

3 dozen mussels in shells
1 teaspoon minced onion
3 slices of bacon, cooked crisp
    and crumbled
½ cup dry white wine

½ teaspoon salt
½ teaspoon paprika
½ teaspoon crumbled dried
    dill

Scrub the mussels and soak in a large pot of seawater or salted water for 2 hours. Discard any that float.

Pour off the water, leaving only a cupful. Cover the pot and steam mussels for 3 minutes, or until shells open. Remove mussels from shells; discard shells. Strain the broth and set aside.

Preheat oven to 325°F.

Place the mussels in a casserole, add the onion, bacon crumbles, wine, strained broth and seasonings. Bake for 15 minutes.

Serve from the casserole, with crusty bread to mop up the broth.

4 servings

DOWN EAST MUSSEL PIE

3 dozen mussels, scrubbed
    and debearded
6 small whole white onions,
    peeled
2 tablespoons butter
¼ teaspoon grated nutmeg

1 teaspoon salt
¼ teaspoon pepper
pinch of dried thyme
pastry for 2-crust 9-inch pie
2 hard-cooked eggs,
    quartered

Preheat oven to 400°F.

Put the mussels in a saucepan, cover with water, bring to a boil, and cook until shells open. Discard any that do not open.

Remove mussels from shells and reserve. Discard shells.

Strain the liquid; add ¾ cup to the onions with butter and seasonings, and simmer until onions are soft but not mushy.

Line a 9-inch pie pan with pastry. Fill pastry with the onions and their liquid, the mussels and the eggs. Cover with the second sheet of pastry, pinch edges, and prick holes in the top for steam vents.

Bake for about 20 minutes, or until browned.

4 servings

CHARCOAL-GRILLED MUSSELS

4 dozen mussels, scrubbed,
    debearded and presoaked
    for 2 hours

melted butter
Parmesan cheese mixed with
    celery seed

Place mussels on a grill over a charcoal fire. When the shells open, remove with tongs to a bowl.

To eat: Remove mussels from shells, dip into melted butter, and sprinkle with cheese mixture.

4 to 6 servings

This recipe may be used also for soft clams.

MUSSELS PROVENÇAL

4 dozen mussels, scrubbed
    and debearded
salt
juice of 1 lemon
½ teaspoon ground saffron
2 tablespoons butter

2 tablespoons flour
4 egg yolks, beaten until
    foamy
croutons
parsley sprigs

Steam mussels in a large kettle with 1 inch of water, 1 teaspoon salt and the lemon juice until shells open. Remove mussels from shells, set aside on a heated platter, and keep warm.

Strain the broth, add the saffron, and boil up for 3 minutes.

Melt the butter in a small saucepan; stir in the flour and some of the broth until smooth. Add to the remaining broth, and bring to a boil. Stir, then allow to cool.

Blend the egg yolks with the cool sauce, stirring constantly. Reheat for about 5 minutes, or until sauce thickens. Season to taste with salt and pour over the mussels. Garnish with croutons and parsley.

4 servings

PAPRIKA MUSSELS

¼ pound butter
3 tablespoons finely chopped
    onion
pinch of dried thyme
¼ bay leaf
3 dozen large mussels (4
    dozen, if small), scrubbed
    and debearded

½ teaspoon salt
½ teaspoon pepper
1 cup dry white wine
2 teaspoons paprika
3 tablespoons Béchamel Sauce
    (see Index)
2 tablespoons heavy cream

Melt the butter in a large saucepan and sauté the onion, thyme and bay leaf for 2 minutes.

Add the mussels, sprinkle with salt and pepper, and pour in the wine. Cover and cook over high heat for 10 minutes.

Remove the mussels, still in their shells, to 4 to 6 heated soup bowls. Strain the liquid.

To the liquid add the paprika, béchamel sauce and cream; stir well. Simmer gently until thickened. Pour sauce over the mussels.

4 to 6 servings

CHEECHAK-DESERTED FARM MUSSELS

20 to 24 large mussels,
    scrubbed and debearded
½ cup dry Chablis or
    Sauterne wine
1 garlic clove, crushed
½ teaspoon salt
6 to 8 peppercorns, crushed

½ teaspoon chopped parsley
¼ teaspoon chopped fresh
    thyme, or pinch of dried
    thyme
3 tablespoons chopped onion
2 tablespoons butter
2 tablespoons flour

Put all ingredients except the butter and flour in a pot and steam until mussel shells open.

Melt the butter in a heavy skillet and stir in the flour to make a roux. Strain the liquid from the mussels and whisk it into the roux until you have a smooth sauce.

Pour the sauce over the mussels. Serve with crisp bread.

2 to 4 servings

FRIED MUSSELS

4 dozen mussels, scrubbed
    and debearded
½ cup olive oil
juice of 1 lemon
2 tablespoons chopped
    parsley

½ teaspoon salt
½ teaspoon white pepper
flour
fat for deep-frying

Place the mussels (only those with tightly closed shells) in a saucepan, cover with water, and cook for 5 minutes, or until shells open.

Remove mussels from the shells and marinate in a mixture of the oil, lemon juice and parsley for 30 minutes.

Drain, season with salt and pepper, and dredge with flour. Fry in deep fat heated to 350°F. on a frying thermometer.

4 servings

OYSTERS

There has long been speculation about—and admiration for—the man who first had the courage to eat an oyster. But there is no doubt that he lived a long time ago, since wall paintings and mosaics made during early Greek and Roman days unmistakably depict the degustation of oysters at banquets and festivals. In all probability, oysters were discovered millennia before then.

In America the first settlers arriving on our shores were delighted to discover large, succulent oysters in great abundance along the coastline.

Oysters do not thrive on the salty ocean floor, but in bays and inlets fed by rivers with fresh water to dilute the salinity and provide food washed down from the land. Commercial marine farmers often plant seedlings in low-salt waters to develop, then transfer them to saltier waters for faster growth. In the warmer waters of the Gulf of Mexico and thereabouts an oyster can grow from seedling to maturity, measuring about 5 inches across the shell, in about a year. "The oyster is the most disinherited of mollusks," Alexander Dumas once said, "Being acephalous—that is to say, having no head—it has no organ of sight, no organ of hearing, no organ of smell . . . neither has it an organ of locomotion. Its only exercise is sleep; its only pleasure, eating." Having no protection against predators except its shell, the oyster seems to have survived only because of its extraordinary fecundity.

The average life-span of an oyster is 3 or 4 years, though in colder waters it may live longer. The most productive areas in the United States are the Chesapeake Bay, the Bayou country of Louisiana, Florida and Long Island waters.

The location of the oyster bed, the salinity, temperature, depth, vegetable and mineral content of the water all play an important role in the coloration, the flavor and size of the oyster and the thickness and conformation of its shell.

Oysters may be gathered as a sport in shallow waters at low tide, but those taken commercially come from cultivated beds. In the Maryland end of the Chesapeake Bay they are tonged or raked from the decks of small boats. Colorful and historic "skipjacks" long have sailed the often stormy waters at this task. Elsewhere larger commercial fleets dredge the sandy bottom throughout the cold winter months.

The oyster shell consists of 2 valves or halves joined together by a powerful hinge which opens and closes them, pumping and filtering food. The lower valve is heavier and more convex. When these shells are tightly closed, all juices are retained. The oyster in its shell, thus, will live out of water for several weeks.

Oysters vary greatly in size. Probably the smallest, the Olympia found in Northern Pacific waters, measures a mere 1½ inches in length of shell. The Caribbean Cupped Oyster found attached to the roots of the mangrove tree is not much larger. On the other extreme, a California oyster transplanted from Japan has a shell often measuring up to a foot across. In between there is a seemingly limitless variety of species, all differing in size, shape and flavor. Chincoteagues, Kent Islands, Patuxents and Tangiers; Blue Points, Lynnhavens and Robins Islands, Cape Cods, Cotuits and Box; Apalachicolas, Indian Rivers, Abascons and Coons (Mangroves); Belons, Chathams, Malpeques and Wellfleets. There are many varieties of oyster in Europe and Japan; the favored kinds in Europe are carefully cultured in small ponds in France, Belgium, Denmark, Holland and Spain; Japan began oyster culture centuries ago.

All of these oysters have a spawning season which usually occurs in late spring during which, though they are safe to eat, they are thin and watery. This season, of course, corresponds to the months with no "R." At all times, oysters are nutritious—rich in proteins, minerals and vitamins. They are easy to prepare, easy to serve, and can be eaten raw, broiled, fried, scalloped, baked or stewed. And oysters have no bones!

How to Buy

Oysters are sold chilled in the shell by the dozen, shucked and iced by the pint or quart. They are also available smoked, canned and frozen. Oysters in the shell when kept chilled travel well and will last for several weeks without spoiling.

How to Prepare

To shuck oysters:

  a. Scrub well under cold running water.
  b. Break off thin end or "bill" with a hammer.
  c. Hold oyster in the palm of one hand with hinge toward heel of palm (better wrap a cloth or towel around hand to protect it).
  d. Force blade of oyster knife between shells at broken end, and twist.
  e. Slice knife down and cut muscle close to upper shell.
  f. Slide knife under oyster, cutting bottom muscle.

How to Store

The valves, or shells, of an oyster, held firmly together by a tough adductor muscle, protect it against predators. This same self-protecting mechanism gives the oyster long life when removed from the sea, and it will remain fresh and succulent for upwards of a month just as long as it remains on ice or in the refrigerator. Once shucked, oysters may be stored in airtight containers, if chilled.

Freezing oysters destroys the flavor.

OYSTER ROAST

Since early colonial days, oyster roasts have been a traditional gustatory activity along the Eastern Seaboard, especially on the Delmarva Peninsula, which hems in the Chesapeake Bay. The popularity of the oyster roast, however, has never quite approached that of the clambake or the crab feast, simply because oysters are not eaten during the warm and festive summer months. Oyster roasts in the fall, however, are still events of considerable social importance.

A bed of white-hot coals is built and covered over with a large grill or grating. The oysters, well scrubbed, are simply dumped onto the grill and roasted until they open.

The hungry guests gather about, spear the oysters with forks, and dip them into melted butter or a hot cocktail sauce made of horseradish, ketchup, Worcestershire and Tabasco. Corn on the cob, sliced tomatoes and baked potatoes accompany the oysters, and all is washed down with mugs of cold beer.

OYSTER BALLS

2 cups warm mashed potatoes	1 teaspoon salt
2 tablespoons butter, warmed	chopped parsley
1 tablespoon lemon juice	1 egg beaten with
1 cup chopped oysters with	1 tablespoon water
their liquor	flour
1 teaspoon dry mustard	oil
dash of Tabasco	

Mix together the potatoes, butter, lemon juice, oysters, seasonings and parsley to taste. Form the mixture into balls about 1 inch in diameter.

Dip the balls into the egg mixture, then roll in flour. Fry, a few at a time, in hot oil until golden brown. Drain, and serve on toothpicks.

4 to 6 servings

BAKED STUFFED OYSTERS

1 dozen large oysters in the shell
4 tablespoons butter
1 tablespoon finely chopped parsley
2 tablespoons finely chopped shallots

1 teaspoon crab seasoning or curry powder
1 teaspoon lemon juice
1 cup fresh bread crumbs

Preheat oven to 400°F.

Shuck the oysters; discard the top shells. Remove and chop the oysters.

Melt the butter; add the oysters and all other ingredients except the crumbs. Spoon into the shells. Sprinkle with crumbs.

Arrange oysters on a bed of rock salt in a shallow baking dish and brown in the oven.

4 servings as first course

OYSTERS ROCKEFELLER

24 large oysters in the shell
1 cup melted butter
¼ cup minced shallots or scallions
¼ cup minced celery
¼ cup minced parsley
1 cup minced watercress or raw spinach
1 garlic clove, minced

few grains of cayenne
½ teaspoon salt
¼ cup fine bread crumbs
1 teaspoon Worcestershire sauce
2 tablespoons sherry wine
¼ cup grated Parmesan cheese
1 lemon, quartered

Scrub the oysters thoroughly. Insert blade of a thin strong knife between edges of shells and pry open by twisting (or have the oysters shucked at the market). Discard the top flatter shells, leaving oysters in curved shells. Run blade of knife under oyster and sever muscle, but leave each oyster in its bottom shell. Arrange oysters on a bed of rock salt in a shallow baking dish.

Preheat oven to 300°F.

Mix together in a blender all the remaining ingredients except the lemon and cheese. Spoon this mixture onto the oysters, sprinkle with cheese, and bake in the oven for 10 minutes, or until golden brown.

Serve with lemon wedges.

4 servings as first course

CAPE COD OYSTER CHOWDER

2 ounces salt pork, diced
1 cup minced onion
2 cups thinly sliced raw
    potatoes
2 cups milk
2 cups light cream
2 tablespoons butter

¼ teaspoon dried thyme
1 teaspoon salt
½ teaspoon freshly ground
    pepper
2 dozen shucked oysters with
    their liquor

Sauté the salt pork in a large pot until crisp. Remove cracklings and reserve.

Add the onion to the pot and sauté for 5 minutes. Do not brown.

Return the cracklings to the pot, add the potatoes, oyster liquor and enough water to cover. Simmer for 20 minutes, or until potatoes are tender.

Add the milk, cream, butter, seasonings and oysters. Simmer over low heat until the edges of the oysters curl. Serve hot with oyster crackers.

4 to 6 servings

NEW ORLEANS OYSTER SOUP

2 ounces salt pork, diced
1½ cups mashed potatoes
2 cups hot milk
1 bouquet garni (bay leaf,
    thyme, parsley)
1 dozen shucked oysters with
    their liquor

1 teaspoon salt
few grains of cayenne
2 slices of French bread,
    toasted

Sauté the salt pork in a heavy pot until crisp. Remove cracklings from the pot and reserve.

Add the potatoes, gradually stir in the milk, then add the *bouquet garni.* Bring almost to a boil, then add the oysters.

When the oysters begin to curl around the edges, remove and discard the *bouquet* and stir in the seasonings.

Serve topped with the salt pork bits, accompanied with toast.

2 servings

OYSTER BISQUE

1 celery rib, chopped
1 onion slice, chopped
1 parsley sprig, chopped
1 bay leaf
2 cups half milk, half cream
2 tablespoons butter

¼ cup flour
1 teaspoon salt
pinch of pepper
1 dozen shucked oysters,
    chopped

Put the celery, onion, parsley, bay leaf and half-and-half in a saucepan, bring almost to a boil, and simmer for 10 minutes. Strain liquid and reserve.

Melt the butter in the top part of a double boiler over simmering water. Stir in the flour and then the liquid and cook until sauce is smooth and thickened.

Add the seasonings and the chopped oysters. Simmer for 2 minutes. Serve in cups.

4 servings

OYSTER VELOUTÉ

2 dozen shucked oysters with
    their liquor
2 cups water
6 tablespoons butter blended
    with 6 tablespoons flour

few dashes of Tabasco
1 teaspoon salt
1 cup heavy cream

Strain the oyster liquor. Put the oysters with their liquor in a heavy saucepan. Add the water and bring almost to a boil, then simmer until the edges of the oysters begin to curl. Remove the oysters with a slotted spoon and keep warm.

Gradually combine the soup with the *beurre manié* (butter and flour), stirring until smooth and thickened. Stir in the seasonings and simmer for 10 minutes.

Add the oysters and cream, simmer for 2 minutes longer, and serve promptly.

4 servings

OLD-FASHIONED OYSTER STEW

2 tablespoons butter
1 teaspoon salt
½ teaspoon white pepper
1 teaspoon celery seeds
    (optional)
2 dozen shucked oysters with
    their liquor

2 cups milk
2 cups light cream
4 pats of butter
4 parsley sprigs, minced

Put butter, seasonings and strained oyster liquor in a pan and bring to a simmer. Add the oysters and cook for about 3 minutes, or until the edges begin to curl. Remove pan from heat.

Heat the milk and cream in a separate pan to just below boiling. Do not boil.

Divide oysters and liquor evenly among 4 hot bowls. Repeat with milk and cream mixture. Garnish each bowl with a pat of butter and minced parsley.

4 servings

This recipe may be used also for Cherrystone clams.

GRAND CENTRAL OYSTER STEW

2 tablespoons butter
1 tablespoon Worcestershire
   sauce
1 teaspoon paprika
½ teaspoon pepper
½ teaspoon celery salt
1 dozen medium-size oysters,
   shucked

1 cup oyster liquor or clam
   broth, or a mixture of the
   two
2 cups milk or half milk, half
   cream
butter
paprika

Heat the top part of a double boiler over boiling water. Put in the butter, Worcestershire and seasonings and cook for a few minutes.

Stir in the oysters and let them froth up for a minute, then pour in the liquor or broth. Boil hard for ½ minute longer. Stir in the milk, bring almost to a boil, and pour quickly into bowls. Garnish with butter and paprika and serve with oyster crackers.

2 servings

This recipe may be used also for Cherrystone clams.

HOT OYSTERS AU BEURRE BLANC

16 large oysters in the shell,
   scrubbed
2 tablespoons dry white wine
1 teaspoon salt

few grains of cayenne
½ cup Beurre Blanc (see
   Index)
minced parsley

Shuck the oysters, reserving their liquor and the bottom shells.

Preheat oven to 350°F.

Place the shells in a shallow baking dish and heat briefly in the oven. Remove and set aside.

Place the oysters with their liquor into a saucepan. Add the wine, salt and cayenne, and cook for about 2 minutes, or until edges of oysters begin to curl. Place an oyster in each of the warm shells.

Cook the liquid down to about 2 tablespoons and spoon over the oysters. Top each with ½ tablespoon beurre blanc and heat briefly in the oven. Serve garnished with parsley.

4 servings

CREAMED OYSTERS, VIRGINIA STYLE

¼ pound butter
½ cup flour
2 cups light cream or milk
1 quart shucked oysters with
their liquor

½ teaspoon salt
¼ teaspoon white pepper
2 tablespoons grated onion
¼ cup sherry wine (optional)

Melt the butter over low heat. Blend in the flour with a wire whisk, add the cream slowly, and cook until sauce is smooth and thickened.

Simmer the oysters in their liquor until the edges curl. Stir the oysters into the sauce; add seasonings, onion and sherry. Heat. Serve on toast or in patty shells.

4 to 6 servings

CHARLESTON BAKED OYSTERS

1 pint shucked oysters with
their liquor
4 tablespoons olive oil
4 tablespoons chopped
shallots
4 tablespoons chopped
parsley
1 garlic clove, minced

½ teaspoon salt
½ teaspoon freshly ground
pepper
dash of Tabasco
1 cup dry white wine
flour
2 tablespoons butter

Preheat oven to 300°F.

Drain the oysters. Reserve the liquor.

Spoon 2 tablespoons olive oil into a shallow baking dish, add the oysters, and then the remaining oil.

Add the herbs, seasonings, wine, and about half of the oyster liquor.

Sift a little flour over the top, and dot with butter. Bake for 15 to 20 minutes, or until brown on top.

Serve with crusty French bread.

4 to 6 servings

SEATTLE OLYMPIA PAN ROAST

1 quart shucked Olympia
   oysters
1 cup chili sauce
1 tablespoon Worcestershire
   sauce

4 tablespoons butter
1 teaspoon salt
½ teaspoon pepper
1 cup light cream
4 slices of crisp toast

Cook the oysters in their own liquor over very low heat for 2 minutes.

Stir in the chili sauce, Worcestershire, butter and seasonings. Bring almost to a boil, then stir in the cream. Serve on toast.

4 servings

OYSTERS À LA KING

1 pint shucked oysters with
   their liquor
4 tablespoons butter
¼ cup chopped celery
¼ cup chopped green pepper
4 tablespoons flour

2 cups milk
1 egg, beaten
1 tablespoon chopped
   pimiento
1 teaspoon salt
¼ teaspoon white pepper

Simmer the oysters in their liquor for about 5 minutes, or until the edges curl. Set aside and keep warm.

Heat the butter in a heavy skillet and sauté the celery and green pepper until tender. Blend in the flour and cook for 2 minutes. Gradually stir in the milk and cook until sauce is smooth and thickened.

Stir a little of the sauce into the beaten egg, then add it to the bulk of the sauce. Keep hot, but do not boil.

Drain the oysters and add to the sauce. Keep liquor for other use. Stir in the pimiento, salt and pepper. Serve on toast or in patty shells.

4 servings

SCALLOPED OYSTERS

1 cup fresh cracker crumbs
1 cup fresh bread crumbs
½ cup melted butter
½ teaspoon salt
¼ teaspoon white pepper

1 pint shucked oysters
½ teaspoon Worcestershire
    sauce
1 cup milk

Preheat oven to 350°F.

Combine the cracker crumbs, bread crumbs, butter and seasonings. Sprinkle one third of this mixture in the bottom of a buttered 6-cup casserole, and cover with half of the oysters. Repeat.

Stir the Worcestershire into the milk and pour milk over the crumbs and oysters. Cover with remaining crumbs. Bake in the oven for 30 minutes, or until brown.

4 to 6 servings

BILOXI OYSTER PIE

4 tablespoons butter
½ cup minced onion
½ cup minced celery
½ cup minced green pepper
1 teaspoon Worcestershire
    sauce

dash of Tabasco
½ teaspoon salt
2 tablespoons flour
2 dozen shucked oysters in
    their liquor
pastry for casserole

Preheat oven to 450°F.

Heat 2 tablespoons butter in a heavy skillet and sauté the onion, celery, green pepper, Worcestershire, Tabasco and salt until vegetables are soft. Do not brown.

Cook the flour in the remaining butter; stir in the oyster liquor until sauce is smooth and thickened. Add the sautéed mixture and the oysters.

Transfer oyster mixture to a buttered 2-quart casserole. Cover with the pastry, crimp the edges, and cut steam vents. Bake in the oven for 15 minutes. Reduce heat to 350°F. and cook for 20 minutes longer.

6 servings

OYSTERS AU GRATIN

6 slices of buttered toast, cut
    into quarters
1 pint shucked oysters
1 cup grated Cheddar cheese
2 eggs, beaten

1 teaspoon salt
1 teaspoon dry mustard
½ teaspoon paprika
½ cup milk

Preheat oven to 350°F.

Place toast pieces in the bottom of a buttered 6-cup casserole. Cover with half of the oysters and one third of the cheese; repeat.

Combine the eggs, seasonings and the milk, and pour over oysters and cheese. Sprinkle remaining cheese on top.

Set casserole in a pan half filled with boiling water. Bake in the oven for 30 minutes, or until brown.

4 to 6 servings

OYSTER PIE WITH MUSHROOMS

1 pint shucked oysters with
    their liquor
¼ pound butter
1 cup small mushrooms, or
    cut-up large mushrooms
1 cup chopped celery
½ cup flour

3 cups milk or light cream
1 teaspoon salt
¼ teaspoon white pepper
pinch of grated nutmeg
few grains of cayenne
pastry for casserole

Preheat oven to 450°F.

Drain the oysters. Reserve the liquor.

Melt the butter in a heavy skillet and cook the mushrooms and celery for 3 minutes. Stir in the flour and gradually add the milk and reserved oyster liquor; cook over low heat, stirring, until sauce is smooth and thickened.

Stir in the oysters and seasonings. Transfer to a 1½-quart casserole. Cover with the pastry, crimp the edges, and cut steam vents. Bake for 15 minutes. Reduce the heat to 325°F. and cook for 20 minutes longer.

4 to 6 servings

This recipe may be used also for soft clams.

LONG ISLAND OYSTER PIE

1 pint shucked oysters with
   their liquor
1 cup thinly sliced onions
1 cup thinly sliced raw
   potatoes
4 tablespoons softened butter
2 tablespoons finely chopped
   parsley

½ teaspoon salt
¼ teaspoon pepper
⅛ teaspoon cayenne
light cream
pastry for casserole

Preheat oven to 450°F.

Drain the oysters. Reserve the liquor.

Arrange a layer of oysters in the bottom of a buttered 1½-quart casserole. Cover with a layer of onions, then a layer of potatoes, half of the butter and seasonings. Repeat.

Add enough cream to the reserved oyster liquor to make ¾ cup, and pour mixture over the casserole. Cover with the pastry, crimp the edges, and cut steam vents.

Bake the pie for 15 minutes. Reduce heat to 350°F. and bake for 20 minutes longer, or until top is brown.

4 to 6 servings

CHARLESTON OYSTER PIE

1 pint shucked oysters with
   their liquor
½ cup tomato juice
2 tablespoons dry sherry wine
½ teaspoon salt

¼ teaspoon pepper
¼ teaspoon grated mace
½ cup melted butter
2 cups cracker crumbs

Preheat oven to 375°F.

Drain the oysters. Strain and reserve the liquor.

Mix together the oyster liquor, tomato juice, sherry and seasonings.

Toss the butter and crumbs together.

Place half of the oysters in a buttered 1½-quart casserole and cover with half of the crumbs. Repeat.

Pour the liquid over all. Bake for 20 minutes, or until brown.

4 servings

OYSTERS CREOLE

1 pint shucked oysters with
    their liquor
4 tablespoons butter
1 tablespoon minced onion
3 large tomatoes, chopped
½ cup chopped celery
2 tablespoons chopped green
    pepper

¼ teaspoon Tabasco
¼ teaspoon chili powder
¼ teaspoon crumbled dried
    tarragon
½ teaspoon salt
1 teaspoon brown sugar
1 tablespoon lemon juice

Drain the oysters and reserve. Strain the liquor and mix with enough water to make 1 cup; reserve.

Melt the butter in a heavy pot and sauté the onion until translucent.

Add the tomatoes, celery, green pepper, seasonings, sugar and lemon juice. Simmer for 10 minutes, then stir in the oyster liquor. Simmer gently, uncovered, for about 30 minutes, or until thickened.

Add the oysters, and cook until edges curl. Serve on rice.

4 to 6 servings

OYSTERS SAINT PIERRE

1 pint shucked oysters with
    their liquor
1 tablespoon butter
1 tablespoon flour
1 cup milk
2 egg yolks, beaten
½ onion, finely chopped
1 tablespoon finely chopped
    parsley

½ cup chopped mushrooms
½ cup finely chopped green
    pepper
½ teaspoon salt
¼ teaspoon pepper
few grains of cayenne
½ cup dry bread crumbs
butter

Preheat oven to 375°F.

Simmer the oysters in their liquor for 5 minutes, or until the edges curl. Drain and chop. Reserve the liquor.

Melt the butter in the top part of a double boiler over simmering water; stir in the flour, then the milk, then the egg yolks and cook until sauce is smooth and thickened.

Add the vegetables, seasonings and reserved oyster liquor. Simmer for 2 minutes, and transfer to a baking dish.

Add the chopped oysters. Sprinkle the top with bread crumbs and dot with butter. Bake for 10 minutes, or until brown.

4 servings

OYSTER CORN PUDDING

1 pint shucked oysters with their liquor	2 cups milk
1 dozen ears of corn	1 teaspoon salt
4 eggs, separated	¼ teaspoon pepper
	2 tablespoons butter, melted

Drain oysters and remove bits of shell. Put oysters in a small saucepan with their liquor and simmer for 2 minutes.

Score ears of corn down the center of each row and cut kernels from cobs. Scrape remaining pulp from the cobs.

Preheat oven to 325°F.

Beat egg yolks until lemon-colored and mix with the corn. Add milk, salt, pepper, melted butter, the oysters and their liquor.

Beat the egg whites until they form limp peaks. Fold egg whites into the oyster-corn mixture.

Butter a 2-quart baking dish and fill with the mixture. Cover lightly with foil. Bake for 50 minutes to 1 hour. There should be a small "jiggle" in the center.

4 to 6 servings

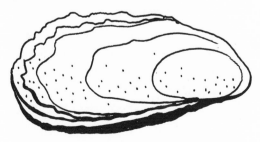

OYSTERS À LA LOUISIANE

4 slices of bacon
2 dozen small oysters,
    shucked and drained
2 tablespoons flour
1½ cups Fish Stock (see
    Index)
1 onion, finely chopped
1 carrot, finely chopped
1 small celery rib, finely
    chopped

½ teaspoon grated lemon rind
1 bay leaf, finely crumbled
2 thyme sprigs, finely
    chopped
2 parsley sprigs, finely
    chopped
¼ cup Madeira wine
½ teaspoon salt
pinch of pepper
few grains of cayenne

Sauté bacon; remove when half cooked. Reserve pan and bacon fat.

Place 6 oysters into each of 4 large ramekins. Cover each one with a slice of bacon. Arrange ramekins in a shallow baking pan and set aside.

Heat the bacon fat. Stir in the flour, cook for 2 minutes, then stir in the stock. Bring to a boil, then add the chopped vegetables, lemon rind and herbs. Simmer, covered, for 20 minutes.

Stir in the Madeira and seasonings. Simmer for a few minutes longer.

Cook the oysters under the broiler until the edges begin to curl and bacon is crisp. Spoon some of the sauce into each ramekin and serve hot.

4 servings

OYSTER FRICASSEE

3 tablespoons butter
½ teaspoon salt
¼ teaspoon pepper
few grains of cayenne

16 medium-size oysters,
    shucked and drained
4 slices of buttered toast
½ cup heavy cream

Melt the butter in a heavy skillet. Add the seasonings and oysters and cook until oysters are plump and the edges begin to curl.

Transfer to 4 heated ramekins, each containing a slice of toast. Keep warm.

Add the cream to the skillet; stir and heat but do not boil. Spoon cream evenly onto the oysters.

4 servings

NORFOLK OYSTER PATTIES

1 pint shucked oysters, well
    drained
8 ounces cream cheese
1 cup cooked rice
2 tablespoons milk
1 egg, beaten
1 tablespoon grated onion

½ teaspoon salt
¼ teaspoon pepper
1 tablespoon sherry wine
1 lemon, half sliced and half
    for juice
1 tablespoon snipped chives

Preheat oven to 350°F.

Chop the oysters. Mix together the oysters, cheese, rice, milk, egg, onion, seasonings and sherry. Form into small patties and place on a baking sheet.

Bake in the oven for 10 minutes, or until golden brown. Sprinkle with lemon juice and chives. Serve hot, garnished with lemon slices.

18 patties

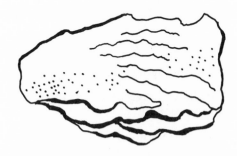

OYSTER CROQUETTES

1 pint shucked oysters with
   their liquor
1 tablespoon butter
2 tablespoons flour
¼ cup heavy cream
2 egg yolks, beaten
2 tablespoons finely chopped
   parsley

½ teaspoon salt
⅛ teaspoon pepper
1 whole egg, beaten
½ cup bread crumbs
2 cups oil for frying

Simmer the oysters in their liquor for 3 to 5 minutes depending on their size. Remove from heat and chop finely.

Melt the butter over low heat. Stir in the flour, then the cream, oysters and liquor. Stir until thickened.

Stir in the egg yolks, parsley and seasonings. Let cool.

Form into 8 small croquettes. Roll each croquette in the beaten egg, then in the bread crumbs.

Fry a few at a time in hot oil, barely smoking (375°F.), until golden brown.

4 servings

DEEP-FRIED OYSTERS

fat for deep-frying
1 quart shucked large oysters
1 cup flour
½ teaspoon salt

⅛ teaspoon pepper
¼ teaspoon grated mace
½ teaspoon baking powder

Preheat fat to 365°F.

Drain the oysters and pat dry with a napkin.

Sift the dry ingredients together. Coat the oysters well, and shake off excess flour.

Place oysters in a frying basket and cook in the hot fat, a few at a time, for 2 to 4 minutes, or until golden brown.

4 to 6 servings

OYSTER FRITTERS

1 dozen shucked oysters with
   their liquor
3 eggs
1 cup sifted flour

½ teaspoon salt
1 cup milk
1 cup bacon fat mixed with
   1 cup peanut oil

Prepare fritter batter 2 hours before use. Drain oysters; strain and reserve liquor. Remove bits of shells; chop oysters.

Beat the egg yolks and whites separately, the yolks until thick and lemon-colored, the whites until stiff.

Stir the oyster liquor into the egg yolks, then add the flour, salt, milk and chopped oysters. Fold in egg whites until incorporated into batter. Refrigerate until ready to use.

Heat the fat and oil in a heavy frying pan to about 375°F. Drop in the batter by the teaspoon, a few at a time. Cook fritters on both sides until brown. Drain and serve immediately.

2 dozen small fritters

This recipe may be used also for quahaugs.

LONG ISLAND OYSTER FRY

1 quart shucked large oysters
1 teaspoon salt
½ teaspoon pepper
2 eggs, lightly beaten
2 tablespoons cream or milk

1 cup bread crumbs, cracker
   crumbs or white
   cornmeal
butter
cooking oil

Drain the oysters, pat them dry with a napkin, and season with salt and pepper.

Mix together the eggs and cream. Dip the oysters into this mixture, then roll them in crumbs.

Heat butter and oil in a heavy skillet to the smoking point. Fry the oysters, a few at a time, until golden brown on both sides.

4 to 6 servings

SCALLOPS

The goddess Venus, born at sea, rode into shore on a scallop shell. If you don't believe it, take a look at Botticelli's great masterpiece painted around 1500. The scallop's fluted valves with radial ribs and wavy outer edges have attracted many artists since earliest times. The graceful, symmetrical shells have appeared regularly in ancient Greek and Roman murals and mosaics, In modern times they have retained this popularity, and show up with consistent frequency in trademarks and colophons.

The scallop, like the oyster and clam, is a bivalve mollusk. But unlike these two that lie immobile on bay bottom and suck in food, the scallop swims through the water and moves along the seabed in search of food. It does this by rapidly opening and clos-

128

ing the shells. Such exercise not surprisingly has the effect of developing the adductor muscle out of all proportion to the creature itself. It is this portion of the scallop that is so prized as food.

There are many species of scallop found up and down the Atlantic Coast and in Pacific waters from the Aleutian Islands to Baja California, all identifiable by differences in size and coloration of shell. For our purpose we will consider only the two principal commercial varieties: Sea Scallops and Bay Scallops.

Bay Scallops, found in shallow waters often hidden in eelgrass, seldom reach a size of more than 3 inches across the shell. They are a great joy to sportsmen who venture forth in the fall wearing old clothes, some wearing waders, all equipped with rakes, pushers, viewers (glass-bottomed boxes), towing along baskets suspended in inner tubes. In Nantucket the month of October is set aside by law for family scalloping in the bay. A bushel basket full is the limit, often reached in a couple of hours if the right spot is found. Then everyone gathers in the little scallop shacks along the shore to see who can shuck his catch fastest. In November, and for the rest of the season, the commercial scallopers take over.

In deep waters commercial scallopers have the ocean to themselves all year and sea scallops are dredged in great numbers. Largely concentrated off the coast of Maine, the industry to a varying degree extends as far south as New Jersey. Due perhaps to the warmer water, scalloping off the California coast has never attained marked importance. In all, sea scallops are more numerous than those found in bays and inlets. They are larger, with shells measuring on the average 5 inches across, and they are delicious to eat, though not quite as sweet and tender as the smaller ones.

How to Buy

Scallops are sold by the pound, packed in ice. Although Europeans eat the entire scallop, in the American market only the adductor muscle is available since the scallop, on being caught and removed from the sea, flutters its shells in an attempt to escape captivity. Unlike oysters and clams, the scallop thus loses its vital juices and quickly spoils. The muscle is therefore removed from the shell immediately after catching and preserved on ice.

Discarded with the rest is the coral, or roe, of the scallop, like a fat orange tongue; the color may be pale or quite vivid. This adds to the attractiveness and flavor of scallop dishes. All European recipes use the roe, along with the scallops or mixed into sauces; if you are following such a recipe, just omit the part using the coral.

How to Prepare

Scallops, as bought in the market, require no prepreparation. As the little boy said, when asked why he liked scallops, "No bones." Be sure they have been washed and wiped very dry before frying or sautéing. And be sure not to overcook. Bays should be sautéed or fried in butter in a sizzling hot pan for no longer than 3 minutes, larger scallops for no longer than 5 minutes.

How to Store

Scallops are almost always marketed raw and iced. They are perishable and must be kept in the refrigerator where they will be safe for at least a week. For longer storage scallops must be frozen, but once thawed should not be refrozen or they run the risk of becoming tasteless.

SCALLOP SEVICHE

2 pounds raw bay scallops, or sea scallops cut into halves
1 tablespoon ground red chile pepper
2 onions, thinly sliced
1 garlic clove, finely chopped
¼ teaspoon freshly ground pepper
1 cup lime juice
1 cup lemon juice

Mix all the ingredients together and place in a deep glass dish so that the scallops are covered with the marinade.

Cover and refrigerate for 4 hours, or until scallops are well "cooked"; they will become opaque as if poached.

Drain and serve on toothpicks as an appetizer.

6 servings

SKEWERED SCALLOPS

6 slices of bacon
24 bay scallops
1 egg, lightly beaten with 1
   cup milk

flour
24 stuffed olives, warmed

Broil the bacon in a heavy skillet until nearly crisp. Remove, cut slices into quarters, and set aside.

Dip the scallops into the egg-milk mixture, dredge with flour, and fry quickly in the bacon fat.

Remove from the skillet and thread alternately onto small wooden picks or skewers with bacon bits and stuffed olives, one of each per skewer.

24 skewers

SCALLOPS IN SHELLS

2 cups bay scallops or cut-up
   sea scallops
6 tablespoons butter
1½ teaspoons salt
½ teaspoon white pepper
1 onion, minced

3 tablespoons flour
1 cup half-and-half
2 tablespoons sherry wine
dry bread crumbs
paprika
1 lemon, quartered

Sauté the scallops in 2 tablespoons butter for not more than 2 minutes, shaking the pan to cook on all sides. Season with 1 teaspoon salt and the pepper, and transfer to 8 buttered scallop shells.

Preheat oven to 250°F.

Sauté the onion in 2 more tablespoons butter until just golden. Stir in the flour and then the half-and-half and cook until mixture thickens. Stir in the sherry, season with ½ teaspoon salt, and spoon sauce over the scallops.

Sprinkle with bread crumbs and paprika, dot with remaining butter, and place in oven until just golden. Serve with lemon wedges at cocktail time or as a first course.

8 cocktail servings, 4 servings as first course

STUFFED AVOCADO

1 cup finely chopped cooked
   scallops
½ cup finely chopped stuffed
   olives
½ cup finely chopped green
   pepper
2 tablespoons Mayonnaise (see
   Index)

few grains of cayenne
2 ripe avocados, halved
   lengthwise, pits removed,
   and brushed with lemon
   juice
8 anchovies

Mix together the first 5 ingredients and spoon into the avocados.
Garnish with crossed anchovies and serve chilled.

4 servings

This recipe may be used also with shrimps, lobster or crab meat.

VERY SPECIAL SCALLOP SOUP

2 medium-size carrots,
   chopped
2 medium-size onions,
   chopped
2 celery ribs, chopped
1 bay leaf
3 tablespoons chopped
   parsley
½ teaspoon freshly ground
   pepper, or a few
   peppercorns

1 cup clam juice, fresh or
   canned
2 cups dry white wine
1 cup water
16 to 20 bay scallops, or 8 sea
   scallops, coarsely
   chopped
snipped chives

Simmer the vegetables and seasonings in the liquids for 30 minutes.

Put the mixture through a sieve, and return the liquid to the pot.

At 4 or 5 minutes before serving add the scallops, simmer for a
few minutes, and serve topped with snipped chives.

4 servings

NANTUCKET SCALLOP CHOWDER

2 cups diced raw potatoes
4 cups milk
1 cup clam broth
1 pint bay scallops
1 teaspoon salt

1 teaspoon pepper
6 sea crackers, toasted
¼ pound salt pork, diced
1 onion, thinly sliced
2 tablespoons butter

Put potatoes into milk and bring to just under a boil. Put clam broth, scallops, salt, pepper and crackers into a large pot or kettle. Add the potatoes and milk.

Sauté the salt pork in a heavy skillet until crisp. Remove the cracklings and set aside. Leave fat in skillet.

Sauté the onion in the pork fat until brown. Add the onion and 1 tablespoon fat to the pot with potatoes and scallops.

Heat for 30 minutes, but do not boil. Stir in the butter and the pork cracklings, and serve.

4 to 6 servings

CURRIED SCALLOP SOUP

1½ pounds bay scallops
2 cups Fish Stock (see Index)
   or clam broth
1 small onion, minced
1 garlic clove, minced
1 tablespoon curry powder

½ teaspoon dried thyme
½ teaspoon freshly ground
   pepper
½ cup heavy cream
2 tablespoons dry sherry wine

Simmer scallops in the stock for 5 minutes. Remove scallops from liquid and set aside.

Add the onion, garlic and seasonings to the stock and simmer for 10 minutes.

Return the scallops and add cream and sherry. Heat, but do not boil. Serve hot or cold.

4 servings

SCALLOP STEW

1 tablespoon butter
1½ pounds fresh scallops, cut
    into halves if large
½ teaspoon salt
½ teaspoon paprika

1 cup milk
1 cup cream
dash of Worcestershire sauce
chopped parsley

Melt the butter in a saucepan, add the scallops, and cook for 3 minutes.

Add remaining ingredients except parsley and cook without boiling for 10 minutes. Serve garnished with parsley.

4 servings

BAKED BAYS, NANTUCKET STYLE

2 cups bay scallops, washed,
    drained and dried
flour
1 cup half-and-half

2 tablespoons butter
1 teaspoon salt
½ teaspoon pepper

Preheat oven to 350°F.

Dredge the scallops with flour and put into a greased 4-cup casserole. Pour on the half-and-half, dot with butter, and season with salt and pepper.

Bake for 30 minutes, and serve from the casserole.

4 servings

OLD-FASHIONED SCALLOP BROIL

1 garlic clove, cut
6 tablespoons butter, melted
1 pound scallops
½ teaspoon salt
½ teaspoon white pepper

few grains of cayenne
flour
1 teaspoon paprika
lemon slices

Rub the bottom and sides of a shallow baking dish or pie pan with the garlic. Add half of the melted butter, and swish it around.

Arrange the scallops in the dish. Season with salt, pepper and a little cayenne, and dust lightly with flour and paprika. Pour on the remaining butter.

Slide under the broiler and cook for 10 minutes, or until scallops are golden. Serve with lemon slices.

4 servings

SCALLOPS EN BROCHETTE

1 pound bay scallops, or
    halved sea scallops
8 slices of bacon, quartered
1 cup mushroom caps
1 garlic clove, crushed

1 scallion, minced
2 tablespoons chopped
    parsley
2 tablespoons olive oil
2 tablespoons butter

Preheat oven to broil, or 500°F.

Thread the scallops, bacon slices and mushrooms alternately on 4 skewers. Cook 3 inches from the source of heat until scallops are opaque on all sides, and the bacon crisp, 3 to 5 minutes.

Meanwhile in a small saucepan gently sauté the garlic, scallion and parsley in the oil and butter, without browning. Dip each skewer into the herb sauce before serving.

Pour the remaining sauce over the skewered scallops.

4 servings

SCALLOPED SCALLOPS

¼ pound butter
1½ cups cracker crumbs
2 eggs, beaten
1 teaspoon salt

½ teaspoon pepper
dash of Tabasco
2 cups bay scallops or halved
    sea scallops

Melt the butter in a saucepan. Stir in the cracker crumbs, eggs and seasonings, and remove from heat.

Preheat oven to 350°F.

Butter a 6-cup casserole and put in the cracker crumb mixture and scallops in alternate layers, with crumbs on top.

Bake for 30 minutes. Serve from the casserole.

4 to 6 servings

SCALLOPS WITH MUSHROOMS

1 pound bay scallops, or sea
    scallops cut up
1 cup clam broth
½ pound mushrooms, cleaned
    and chopped
4 tablespoons butter

2 tablespoons flour
1 cup milk
1 teaspoon salt
pinch of cayenne
1 lemon, cut

Simmer the scallops gently in the clam broth for 3 to 5 minutes. Drain, reserving the broth.

Sauté the mushrooms in 2 tablespoons butter for 5 minutes. Stir in the flour and cook for 3 minutes longer. Stir in the milk and seasonings and cook until sauce is thickened. Add some of the reserved broth if necessary to give sauce correct texture.

Melt remaining 2 tablespoons butter and stir it and the scallops into the mushroom sauce.

Pile into 4 scallop shells, squeeze a little lemon juice onto each, and serve.

4 servings

SCALLOPS IN WINE

2 tablespoons butter
2 tablespoons olive oil
2 pounds fresh sea scallops
½ teaspoon salt
½ teaspoon white pepper

½ teaspoon paprika
1 cup fine dry bread crumbs
½ cup dry white wine
snipped fresh dill

Heat the butter and oil in a heavy skillet. Dry the scallops and season with salt, pepper and paprika; dust lightly with bread crumbs.

Sauté the scallops over high heat for 5 minutes, turning them to brown evenly. Do not overcook. Remove to a heated platter.

Stir the wine into the pan juices, simmer for a minute, and pour over the scallops. Serve garnished with snipped dill.

4 servings

SCALLOPS NEWBURG

1 pound scallops
2 tablespoons butter
½ teaspoon paprika
1 teaspoon salt
½ cup Madeira or sherry wine

2 cups half-and-half
2 tablespoons flour
2 egg yolks
8 toast points

Sauté the scallops gently in butter for a few minutes (longer for sea scallops). Add seasonings and wine.

Mix 1 cup of the half-and-half with the flour until smooth, then add the second cup. Stir into the scallops until mixture thickens.

Remove from heat, stir in the egg yolks, and spoon onto toast points.

4 servings

NEW ENGLAND SCALLOP PIE

2 pounds fresh sea scallops,
    cut into halves across the
    grain
1 small onion, thinly sliced
2 medium-size raw potatoes,
    thinly sliced
1 bay leaf
½ teaspoon salt

½ teaspoon pepper
few grains of cayenne
pinch of ground sage
½ cup half cream, half milk
2 tablespoons Fish Stock (see
    Index) or clam broth
pastry for top of casserole

Preheat oven to 350°F.

In a well-buttered shallow 2-quart casserole arrange the scallops, onion and potatoes in alternate layers with the bay leaf in the center.

Sprinkle with the seasonings and pour in the half-and-half and the stock or broth.

Cover with the pastry, press edges firmly, and cut steam vents. Bake in the oven for 30 to 40 minutes, or until crust is golden and juice comes through the vents.

6 servings

BROILED SCALLOPS WITH MUSHROOMS

2 pounds fresh sea scallops,
  cut into halves across the
  grain
1 cup water containing 2
  tablespoons salt
2 tablespoons butter
½ pound mushrooms,
  coarsely chopped
1 tomato, diced

1 small onion, diced
1 tablespoon minced parsley
1 teaspoon salt
½ teaspoon pepper
1 cup Béchamel Sauce (see
  Index)
paprika
minced parsley

Boil the scallops in the salted water for 2 minutes. Drain and chop into small pieces but do not mince. Reserve.

Preheat broiler. Have ready 6 large scallop shells or coquilles.

Melt the butter in a saucepan and sauté the mushrooms for 10 minutes. Add the tomato, onion, parsley, salt and pepper. Simmer over low heat for 10 minutes.

Mix in the chopped scallops and Béchamel sauce.

Spoon into the scallop shells, and sprinkle with paprika. Brown under the broiler. Garnish with parsley.

6 servings

DEVILED SCALLOPS

3 tablespoons butter
½ teaspoon dry mustard
½ teaspoon salt
few grains of cayenne
½ cup Fish Stock (see Index)
  or clam broth

2 pounds fresh sea scallops,
  chopped
cracker crumbs
butter

Preheat oven to 375°F. Have ready 4 large scallop shells or coquilles.

Cream together the butter, mustard and seasonings. Add the stock and chopped scallops and mix. Spoon into scallop shells or coquilles, sprinkle with cracker crumbs, and dot with butter.

Place shells on a baking sheet and bake in the oven for 20 minutes.

4 servings

COQUILLES SAINT-JACQUES

1½ pounds fresh scallops, cut
  into halves if large
1 tablespoon chopped shallot
½ teaspoon salt
pinch of white pepper

½ cup dry white wine or dry
  vermouth
1 tablespoon flour blended
  with 3 tablespoons butter
1 cup cream
minced parsley

Preheat oven to 400°F. Have ready 4 large scallop shells or coquilles.

Put the scallops, shallot, seasonings and wine into a saucepan. Bring to a boil, reduce heat, cover, and simmer for 2 minutes.

Remove scallops and divide into the shells or coquilles.

Cook the liquid remaining in the saucepan over high heat until reduced to half.

Stir in the flour-butter mixture (*beurre manié*). Stir in the cream and continue cooking to thicken the sauce. Pour sauce over the scallops.

Place coquilles on a baking sheet. Bake in the oven for 5 minutes. Garnish with parsley and serve piping hot.

4 servings

SCALLOPS IN VELOUTÉ SAUCE

2 tablespoons butter
4 tablespoons flour
2 cups Fish Stock (see Index)
1 teaspoon salt

½ teaspoon pepper
2 cups bay scallops or halved
  sea scallops
2 tablespoons heavy cream

Heat the butter, stir in the flour, and cook for a few minutes without browning. Whisk in the stock and seasonings until smooth and thickened.

Stir in the scallops and continue cooking over very low heat for 3 minutes. Remove from heat and stir in the cream. Serve at once.

4 servings

This recipe may be used also for lobster meat, crab meat, shrimps or almost any other shellfish.

BAKED SCALLOPS AU GRATIN

4 tablespoons butter
1 cup sliced mushrooms
2 celery ribs, chopped
1 small onion, chopped
½ green pepper, chopped
½ teaspoon salt
pinch of dried basil

1 pound fresh scallops, cut
   into halves if large
2 cups Béchamel Sauce (see
   Index)
½ cup cracker crumbs
½ cup grated cheese
butter for topping

Preheat oven to 325°F.

Melt the butter in a saucepan. Stir in the vegetables and seasonings and simmer for 5 minutes.

Add the scallops and cook for 3 minutes longer.

Stir in the Béchamel sauce. Pour the mixture into a buttered 6-cup casserole. Sprinkle with cracker crumbs, then with cheese. Dot with butter.

Bake in the oven for 20 minutes, or until brown on top.

4 servings

SCALLOP FRY

fat for deep-frying
2 pounds bay scallops, or sea
   scallops sliced into halves
   across the grain, fresh or
   frozen (not thawed)
½ teaspoon salt
½ teaspoon white pepper

2 eggs, beaten
few grains of cayenne
pinch of grated mace or
   nutmeg
cracker crumbs
Tartar Sauce (see Index)

Preheat fat to 375°F. on a frying thermometer.

Dry the scallops well and season with salt and pepper.

Dip scallops into the eggs, which have been beaten with the cayenne and mace. Roll them in cracker crumbs.

Fry in hot fat for 2 to 3 minutes for fresh, 3 to 4 minutes for frozen.

Serve with tartar sauce.

4 servings

Part Three

UNIVALVE
MOLLUSKS

ABALONES
CONCHS AND WHELKS
PERIWINKLES
SNAILS
SEA URCHINS
OCTOPUSES
SQUIDS

ABALONES

The abalone is a univalve mollusk, a one-shell shellfish, whose shell protects it from above as it clings or moves about with its one large foot below. The shell, ear-shaped and embellished with a neat row of holes, attains a growth of about 12 inches and is of greater value even than the meat it protects. The rich opalescent coloration of the lining—greens, blues, pinks, ivories—offers unusual attraction for the jewelry industry. The meat itself is tough and rubbery but, when tenderized, it yields delicately flavored steaks.

There are many species of abalone found in the shallow waters along the coasts of Asia and Africa, and in the Mediterranean Sea. Several important varieties appear along the Pacific Coast,

143

from California to Mexico to Chile, but no abalone of importance has ever shown up along our Atlantic Coast.

In California the supply has been so depleted by early shipments to Japan and by the voracious appetite of sea otters, that abalone has almost become an endangered species and is protected by state legislation. Shipping abalone, fresh or frozen, canned or dried, out of the state is strictly forbidden. Following in the footsteps of Japan, a great deal of effort has gone into the development of abalone farms, though production on a commercial scale may be a few years away.

How to Buy

Abalones are scarce in almost all of the United States. What little abalones are carried in specialty markets come from Mexico or Japan, usually dried, frozen or canned in slices or cubes.

How to Prepare

In the unlikely event that you should find yourself in possession of a fresh or live abalone, here's what you do: Cut meat from shell, discard viscera, trim away dark-colored mantle, and remove skin from foot. Slice into ⅜-inch-thick steaks. Pound steaks gently with a wooden mallet or rolling pin. Sauté in hot butter for no more than 45 seconds on each side, or eat raw with a squeeze of lime juice.

How to Store

Frozen abalone meat, the only kind most people are likely to encounter, will keep in the freezer for a month or longer. Once thawed, however, this delicately flavored seafood should not be refrozen.

ABALONE SEVICHE

1 pound fresh abalone meat, cut into ½-inch-thick slices
1 cup fresh lime juice
1 tablespoon minced chives or scallions

1 tablespoon minced parsley
dash of Tabasco
2 tablespoons olive oil
½ teaspoon salt

Pound the abalone slices, cut up into 1-inch squares, and marinate in the lime juice for 4 hours.

Drain. Add the remaining ingredients, mixing thoroughly. Serve on toothpicks.

4 servings

ABALONE SOUP

1 pound abalone meat, fresh, canned or thawed frozen
2 cups hot water
3 cups light cream
2 tablespoons butter
pinch of grated nutmeg
½ teaspoon salt
1 teaspoon sherry wine

Cut the abalone into ½-inch-thick slices, pound the slices, and cut into ¼-inch cubes.

Simmer in 2 cups water for 3 minutes. Remove cubes and reserve. Boil the liquid over high heat and reduce to half.

Add the cream, butter, nutmeg and salt to reduced liquid. Simmer for 1 minute, then add the abalone bits and the sherry. Heat and serve. Or serve chilled.

4 servings

This recipe may be used also for conchs or whelks.

PANBROILED ABALONE STEAKS

2 pounds abalone, trimmed and cut into ½-inch-thick steaks
juice of 2 lemons
1 teaspoon paprika
1 teaspoon chopped parsley
2 teaspoons butter

Pound abalone steaks, then marinate them in the lemon juice mixed with paprika and parsley for 1 hour.

Melt the butter in a heavy skillet. Add the steaks and panbroil for 1 minute on each side, or until golden.

Serve with Béarnaise Sauce (see Index).

4 servings

This recipe may be used also for conchs or whelks.

ABALONE CHOWDER

1 pound abalone meat, fresh,
    canned or thawed frozen
1 quart water
pinch of dried thyme
dash of Tabasco
1 teaspoon salt

¼ pound salt pork, diced
1 onion, chopped
3 raw potatoes, peeled and
    cubed
2 cups milk or half-and-half
3 tablespoons butter
chopped parsley

Trim the abalone, if necessary, and put in a saucepan with the water, thyme, Tabasco and salt. Cover and boil for 1 hour. Remove abalone from the broth, chop, and return to the broth.

In a skillet sauté the pork and onion until golden; add to the broth.

Add potatoes to the broth and simmer for 20 minutes, or until potatoes are tender.

Stir in the milk and butter. Check seasoning. Serve garnished with parsley.

4 servings

ABALONE IN CASSEROLE

2 pounds abalone meat, fresh,
    canned or thawed frozen
2 tablespoons butter
1 onion, chopped
1 garlic clove, crushed

1 tablespoon tomato paste
1 teaspoon prepared mustard
½ cup chopped parsley
1 tablespoon lemon juice
1 cup water

Preheat oven to 350°F.

Cut the abalone meat into ½-inch-thick slices and pound slices with a mallet. Cut into bite-size portions and put in a buttered casserole.

Melt the butter in a heavy skillet and sauté the onion and garlic. Stir in the tomato paste, mustard, parsley, lemon juice and water. Simmer for 5 minutes. Add sauce to the casserole and bake in the oven for 1 hour.

6 servings

This recipe may be used also for conchs or whelks.

FRIED ABALONE

2 pounds abalone meat, fresh,
    canned or thawed frozen
1 teaspoon salt
½ teaspoon pepper

2 eggs, beaten
1 cup fine dry bread crumbs
½ cup olive oil

Cut the abalone meat into ½-inch-thick slices and pound slices with a mallet.

Wipe the slices dry. Sprinkle with salt and pepper, dip into beaten eggs, and then into bread crumbs.

Heat the oil in a heavy skillet and brown the abalone slices for 1½ minutes on each side.

4 to 6 servings

ABALONE SALAD

1 pound abalone meat, fresh,
    canned or thawed frozen
salad greens
1 tablespoon olive oil
1 teaspoon lemon juice

2 celery ribs, chopped
1 tomato, sliced
½ green pepper, sliced
Mayonnaise (see Index)

Cut the abalone meat against the grain into ½-inch-thick slices. Pound slices and cut into ½-inch pieces.

Wash and drain the salad greens. Shred greens and toss with the oil and lemon juice.

Arrange greens on 4 plates. Spoon abalone bits onto each plate, surround with chopped celery and tomato and green pepper slices, and top with mayonnaise.

4 servings

CONCHS
AND
WHELKS

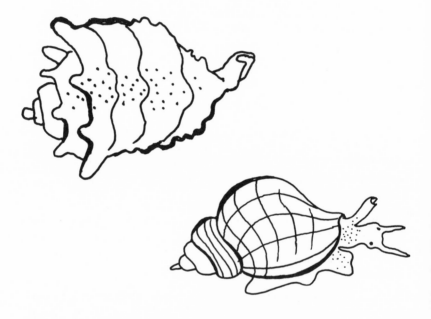

These two mollusks have emerged from entirely different strains of the gastropod family. They live in different areas of the world—conchs (pronounced konks) in the warmer waters of the Caribbean, the waters surrounding the South Pacific islands and those off California; whelks in those of the North Atlantic from Maine to New Jersey, and in the Mediterranean Sea. But they are both snails spending their lives inside of heavy spiraled shells and moving about on a powerful muscular foot. This foot, the edible portion of both animals, is very similar in texture, flavor and the creamy-white color. In fact, conchs and whelks are so similar in so many ways that it seems reasonable to treat them almost as the

148

same shellfish. Clearly, any recipe that will serve for a conch will serve also for a whelk.

As an industry, fishing for conchs and whelks does not amount to very much except in the Caribbean and off the shores of California. A fair amount are gathered by scuba divers; some are found entangled in the nets of fishermen as they go for other more lucrative catches.

How to Buy

Conchs and whelks are sold live in the shell in fishmarkets near their habitat. In New York, Boston and San Francisco they are sold as *scungilli,* a favorite food of Italian and other Mediterranean gastronomes. They may be found dressed and chilled or frozen. The meat, cut into chunks or strips, is canned. Conch is plentiful in the markets of Key West and Caribbean cities.

How to Prepare

To remove the meat from the shell, place open side down and break a hole in the shell with a hammer at the third spiral, exposing the muscle that attaches the body. Sever the muscle with a sharp knife and let the body drop out. Cut away and discard the viscera and operculum, leaving the large foot which must now be skinned, pounded until tender, then cut into slices or put through a meat grinder, depending upon the use you plan for it.

This method of removing the meat at the same time destroys the shell. If the shell is desired as a decorative souvenir, the body must be destroyed and removed. The usual practice is to pour in a little acetic acid and let stand until the meat drops out.

How to Store

Conchs and whelks in the shell may be kept on ice for a week or more, just as long as the operculum is intact and closed. Beware if the shells begin to lose their life-sustaining liquids. The meat, once removed from the shell, must be iced or frozen and it will last for weeks.

CONCH OR WHELK SEVICHE

1 pound fresh conch or whelk
   meat
juice of 2 limes
2 tablespoons olive oil

1 teaspoon salt
few grains of cayenne
1 pimiento, diced
½ green pepper, diced

Pound the meat with a mallet and cut into thin ¾-inch squares. Add the lime juice, oil, seasonings, pimiento and green pepper. Cover and marinate for 3 hours, stirring occasionally.

Serve in the marinade, with toothpicks.

4 servings

KEY WEST CONCH CHOWDER

1 pound conch meat, fresh,
   thawed frozen or canned
1½ cups water
½ cup dry white wine
¼ pound salt pork, diced
1 onion, chopped
2 raw potatoes, peeled and
   cubed

2 cups half-and-half
3 tablespoons butter
dash of Tabasco
1 teaspoon salt
½ teaspoon pepper
minced parsley

Pound conch meat and cut into ½-inch dice. Put the dice in a pot with the water and wine. Simmer for 5 to 6 minutes. Let stand.

Sauté the pork and onion in a heavy skillet until golden. Add the potatoes and 1½ cups cooking liquid from the conch. Simmer for 15 minutes, or until potatoes are tender.

Add conch meat to the pot, stir in the half-and-half, and add the butter and seasonings. Bring chowder to serving temperature. Serve garnished with parsley.

4 servings

This recipe may be used also for whelks.

CONCH STEW WITH MUSHROOMS

2 pounds conch meat, fresh
    or thawed frozen, cut into
    ¾-inch-thick slices
3 tablespoons butter
1 tablespoon cooking oil
1 teaspoon dry mustard
1 teaspoon salt

½ teaspoon pepper
1 tablespoon vinegar
½ cup hot water
1 tablespoon flour
1 cup sliced raw mushrooms
toast

Pound the conch slices with a wooden mallet, and cut into pieces. Sauté in 2 tablespoons butter and the oil for 7 minutes on each side.

Add the seasonings, vinegar and water. Cover and simmer for 30 minutes.

Remove the conch and chop into small pieces; discard the liquid or reserve for another dish.

Heat remaining tablespoon of butter; stir in the flour and let it brown. Stir in the conch pieces and the mushrooms, and cook for 3 minutes.

Serve on toast.

4 servings

This recipe may be used also for whelks.

PANBROILED CONCH STRIPS

1½ pounds conch meat, fresh
    or thawed frozen
½ teaspoon salt
½ teaspoon white pepper

flour
2 tablespoons olive oil
minced parsley

Cut the conch across the grain into ½-inch-thick slices. Pound slices with a mallet. Slice into strips of manageable size. Sprinkle with salt and pepper; dust with flour.

Heat the oil in a heavy skillet and panbroil the conch strips for about 2 minutes on each side, or until brown and crisp. Garnish with parsley.

4 servings

This recipe may be used also for whelks.

FRIED CONCH STEAKS

oil for deep-frying
1½ pounds conch meat, fresh
   or thawed frozen
1 egg, beaten with 1 cup milk

dry bread crumbs
salt and pepper
4 lemon wedges

Preheat oil to 365°F. on a frying thermometer.

Cut the conch into ½-inch-thick slices and pound with a mallet. Cut slices into steaks of manageable size.

Dip the steaks into the egg-milk mixture, then into the bread crumbs. Place steaks, a few at a time, in a wire basket and fry for 3 to 4 minutes, or until golden.

Drain, season with salt and pepper, and serve at once with lemon wedges.

4 servings

This recipe may be used also for whelks.

CONCH FRITTERS

oil for deep-frying
2 cups finely chopped conch
   meat, fresh, thawed
   frozen or canned
2 cups water
1 cup flour
1 teaspoon baking powder

1 teaspoon salt
½ teaspoon white pepper
2 eggs, beaten
1 cup milk
1 tablespoon finely chopped
   onion

Preheat oil to 365°F. on a frying thermometer.

Cook the chopped conch in the 2 cups water for 10 minutes. Drain conch and set both conch and liquid aside.

Sift together the flour, baking powder and seasonings. Mix in the eggs and then the milk, drained conch and chopped onion. Add as much of the cooking liquid as needed to give correct texture to the batter; it should not be too thin. Whisk well.

Drop batter by spoonfuls into the hot oil and cook for about 6 minutes, or until golden on all sides.

4 servings

This recipe may be used also for whelks.

PERIWINKLES

These are small mollusks with spiraled snaillike shells found in large colonies in tidal waters and brackish pools. In the United States their habitat seems to be limited to the East Coast. Sometimes, following a storm at sea, the beaches will be littered with the little 1-inch tidbits and they can be gathered in baskets.

How to Buy

In eastern markets, when found, they are displayed in bushel baskets and sold by the pound. Although caught year-around, the peak season is July and August.

153

How to Prepare

These little snails of the sea, unlike their terrestrial cousins, escargots, have clean eating habits and therefore do not require starving before cooking. Merely rinse several times and heat in a little salted water. The sealing membrane, called the operculum, breaks and the little animals retreat farther into their shells whence with a little patience they may be removed with a toothpick. Simmer them for a minute or so and prepare them like snails.

How to Store

Live periwinkles may be kept on ice for a week or more. They must be contained, however, or they will crawl away.

WINKLES IN THE SHELL

6 dozen periwinkles, washed in cold water
salt
6 ounces butter, softened

½ cup minced parsley
2 garlic cloves, minced
oil

Boil the periwinkles in salted water for 5 minutes. Cool. Remove the meat from the shells with a toothpick and rinse in cold water.

Cream the butter with the parsley, garlic and 1 teaspoon salt.

Oil the insides of 32 shells and stuff each with 3 periwinkles. Fill with the garlic butter.

Arrange butter side up in a shallow baking dish and let stand for 2 hours.

Preheat oven to 250°F.

Bake periwinkles in the oven for 10 minutes. Serve with toothpicks.

4 servings

PERIWINKLES ON STICKS

6 dozen fresh periwinkles, washed in cold water
salt

Drawn Butter or Supreme Cocktail Sauce (see Index)

Boil the periwinkles in salted water for 5 minutes. Drain, and remove to a bowl.

Serve with toothpicks.

Let your guests remove the winkles from the shells and dip into butter or sauce.

4 servings

VENETIAN RISOTTO

6 dozen periwinkles
salt
4 tablespoons olive oil
2 garlic cloves, finely chopped
1 tablespoon chopped parsley

1 cup dry white wine
¼ teaspoon pepper
2 cups uncooked rice
6 cups Fish Stock (see Index), hot

Boil the periwinkles in salted water for 5 minutes. Cool. Remove the meat from the shells with a toothpick and rinse with cold water.

Heat the oil and sauté the garlic and parsley. Add the periwinkles and sauté for 2 minutes longer. Add the wine, 1 teaspoon salt and the pepper.

Stir in the rice and cook until golden. Stir in 1 cup of the stock and simmer until absorbed. Continue adding stock by the cupful until all has been absorbed. Serve immediately.

4 servings

This recipe may be used also for small clams or cut-up snails.

SNAILS

One species or another of snails is found literally everywhere—on land and in the sea. Many varieties are edible although they might not have the greatest flavor, or they might be too small to bother with. Those identified by the French as *escargots* usually belong to a class called *petits gris* and are raised not only in France and Switzerland but also in Turkey, Greece, Japan, Taiwan and North Africa. A very special *escargot* called *grand blanc* is cultivated in the Burgundy wine country and is fed on grape leaves.

Snails, it would seem, are very easy to grow (in fact are considered pests in many areas of the world), but the actual cultivation of edible snails requires considerable attention and know-how. After harvesting, they must first be starved for at least 48 hours to

156

purge them of any food they might have ingested—food harmless to themselves but poisonous or unpleasant to humans.

Like conchs, whelks and periwinkles, snails live their entire lives in their spiraled shells, retreating for protection and emerging only halfway to feed. They are very active, moving about slowly but persistently on a well-formed foot, lubricated by a viscous mucous.

How to Buy

Snails are sold live in the shell to a limited degree in many big-city markets. You buy them by the dozen. Canned snails are plentiful in specialty stores, smaller varieties packed 2 dozen to the can, larger ones about 12 to the can. Packaged shells are sold separately, as are porcelain imitations. You can also purchase special metal or ceramic snail plates with depressed cups to hold the snails, metal tongs and little two-pronged forks, all to make the ritual of eating snails more exciting.

How to Prepare

Live snails, before cooking, should be starved for about 48 hours, just in case they haven't been purged before reaching the market. Then observe the following simple procedure: Place snails in a deep kettle, cover with cold water, and soak for 30 minutes, covering the kettle to prevent their escape. Drain. Discard any snails whose heads have not emerged from the shell. To cook, cover with salt water and simmer for 5 minutes, or until snails have retreated into the shell and operculum has broken. Remove from the shell with a nutpick and cut off the heads and tails.

Canned snails, the kind you are most likely to encounter, do not of course require all the precautionary treatment of live snails. They have already been purged and cooked. However, to remove the ever-present canned taste it is advisable to poach them in a little salted water, or white wine, before following the recipe.

How to Store

Canned snails, of course, present no storage problem. But live snails may become a nuisance as they are apt to wander all over the kitchen. Keep them in a basket (they need to breathe), but be sure there is a securely fastened lid.

BAKED SNAILS

1 cup dry white wine
½ cup water
1 teaspoon salt
few peppercorns
24 small or 12 large (halved)
    canned snails
6 tablespoons butter
1 garlic clove, minced

¼ pound fresh mushrooms,
    sliced
1 teaspoon minced parsley
½ teaspoon freshly ground
    pepper
½ teaspoon salt
dry bread crumbs
butter

Preheat oven to 400°F. Have ready 4 ramekins.

Heat the wine, water, salt and peppercorns, and poach the snails for 10 minutes. Drain. Place snails in the ramekins. Reserve the poaching liquid.

Melt the butter and sauté the garlic, mushrooms, parsley and seasonings for about 5 minutes.

Add the reserved liquid and simmer for 5 minutes longer.

Pour the sauce evenly into the ramekins. Top with bread crumbs and dot with butter. Bake in the oven for 7 to 8 minutes, or until browned.

4 servings

SNAILS BURGUNDY STYLE

24 small or 12 large (halved)
    canned snails, with shells
1 cup dry white wine
1 cup water
4 tablespoons unsalted butter,
    softened

1 garlic clove, minced
1 tablespoon minced shallot
¼ cup minced parsley
½ teaspoon salt
½ teaspoon freshly ground
    pepper

Preheat oven to 425°F. Have ready 24 well-scrubbed snail shells.

Poach the snails in the wine and water for 3 minutes. Drain. Stuff the snails into the shells.

Cream the butter with the garlic, shallot, parsley and seasonings, and use the butter to plug up the openings in the shells.

Place in special snail dishes or in a shallow baking dish. Bake in the oven for 10 minutes.

4 servings

ANCHOVY SNAILS

24 small or 12 large (halved) canned snails, with shells
1 cup water
1 teaspoon salt
1 cup dry bread crumbs
6 anchovy fillets, minced
1 teaspoon chopped onion
2 teaspoons minced parsley
½ teaspoon freshly ground pepper
1 egg, beaten
2 tablespoons melted butter
snipped dill
1 cup Béchamel Sauce (see Index), optional

Preheat oven to 425°F. Have ready 24 well-scrubbed snail shells.

Poach the snails in salted water for 10 minutes. Drain, chop, and reserve.

Mix together the bread crumbs, anchovy fillets, onion, parsley, pepper, beaten egg and butter.

Add the reserved chopped snails; mix well. Stuff the mixture into the shells.

Place in a shallow baking dish. Bake in the oven for 7 to 8 minutes. Serve garnished with dill.

Provide a dish of béchamel sauce for dipping.

4 servings

SNAILS WITH MUSHROOMS

24 small or 12 large (halved)
    canned snails
1 cup water
1 teaspoon salt
3 tablespoons olive oil
¼ pound fresh mushrooms,
    diced
½ onion, minced
1 garlic clove, minced

1 teaspoon minced parsley
pinch of dried rosemary
½ teaspoon salt
½ teaspoon freshly ground
    pepper
½ cup dry white wine
4 slices of French bread,
    toasted
minced parsley

Poach the snails in the salted water for 10 minutes. Drain; reserve snails and discard poaching liquid.

Heat 1 tablespoon olive oil in a small saucepan and sauté the mushrooms for 10 minutes. Remove and reserve.

Heat 2 tablespoons olive oil and sauté the onion, garlic, parsley, rosemary and seasonings for 5 minutes, or until onion is golden.

Add the reserved snails and mushrooms and simmer gently for 30 minutes.

Add the wine, and simmer for 5 minutes longer. Pour over individual servings of toast and garnish with parsley.

4 servings

SEA URCHINS

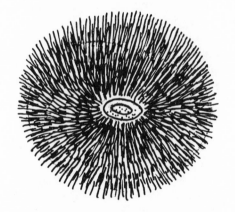

The Sea Urchin is a member of the family of echinoderms, which also includes the starfish and the sea cucumber.

This egg-shaped mollusk, round on top and flattened on the bottom, is entirely covered with stiff, sharp spines. It ranges in size from 1½ inches to as large as 8 to 10 inches across, and varies in color from purple to green, to brown, to black, depending upon the species and locale of habitat. It is a voracious eater and much feared by the other inhabitants of the ocean bottom.

The sea urchin is found almost everywhere—in tidal pools, reefs, along pebbly shores and in deep waters—in the Mediterranean,

161

along the East and West Coasts of the Americas, in the Caribbean Sea.

Sea Urchins enjoy a limited popularity even in Europe, the Orient, the Caribbean and Chile, but those admirers that do exist consider them a great delicacy and are avid eaters, consuming them by the dozen. Sea urchins seldom, if ever, show up on a restaurant menu. Their popularity seems to be limited to a between-meal treat and, at least to some, as an aphrodisiac, probably because the portions that are eaten are the gonads and the roe.

How to Buy

Sea Urchins are perishable in warm weather and therefore are rarely available except during the winter months, and even then only in the larger fish markets of cities like New York, San Francisco and Boston, supplied sometimes by scuba divers who rake them from the ocean floor into wire cages, and by fishermen who find them entangled in their nets.

How to Prepare

Cook in salted water briefly, for 2 to 3 minutes. Cool, then cut around the bottom (flat) side of shell with kitchen shears or a sharp knife. Better wear gloves. Remove bottom shell and shake out viscera. Roe or gonads, cream or orange in color, can be dipped out and eaten with a spoon or scooped up with crusty French bread. The female ovaries are more egglike; the male gonads have a finer texture.

How to Store

The only way that sea urchins are sold is live, usually stored on a bed of iced seaweed. After purchase they should be kept in the same manner. But sea urchins are perishable and it is advisable to consume them within a week.

OCTOPUSES

The Octopus, along with the squid and cuttlefish, is a member of the Cephalopod class of mollusks, although its shell, with the exception of the beak, has been phased out by evolution. One of the most highly organized of all marine creatures, it has the largest and best functioning brain of any invertebrate animal. It swims with great rapidity by jet propulsion, emits a smoke screen of "ink" to confound enemies, and has the ability to change color to match its environment—even gets red in the face when angered. The octopus uses tools—sticks and stones—to pry loose an abalone or crack open a clam.

The octopus is a frightening creature in appearance, with a globular body, unblinking, staring eyes and 8 long tentacles covered with suction cups; little wonder that it is so often cast as villain in movie and TV shows. But not to worry. This animal never reaches the imposing proportions of fiction. Rather, it averages, at least commercially, around 2 or 3 pounds.

The Japanese, Spanish, Portuguese, Italians and Greeks constitute the principal cephalopod lovers of the world. In the United States gastronomic appreciation is pretty much limited to their descendants. Although octopuses abound along the shores of both coasts, most of the commercial catch is made in the Pacific from Alaska south to Baja California and around the Hawaiian Islands.

About 80 percent of the octopus is esculent. The meat is white, firm, sweet and tender (only poor cooking renders it tough).

How to Buy

Octopuses are sold in selected markets and Japanese stores along both coasts of the United States. They usually appear fresh or frozen, skinned and with viscera, beak and eyes removed. Sometimes they may be bought precooked. Frozen octopuses, packaged in 2-pound and 10-pound boxes, are imported from Spain. Dried octopus meat, and smoked meat too, may sometimes be found in specialty shops, as well as octopus in cans.

How to Prepare

In almost all cases the octopus you buy in the market will already have been thoroughly dressed and skinned. Should you be confronted with the task of preparing an octopus, first wash it in salted water, then cut away the beak and eyes and remove the viscera and outer skin. To skin, dip several times into boiling water, then peel the skin from body and tentacles. Tenderize large octopuses by pounding with a mallet or flat object until soft. Octopus meat is best when cooked either very briefly or for a long time.

How to Store

Octopus should be stored in the frozen state in which it was purchased. Do not thaw until ready for cooking. Once thawed, refreezing octopus diminishes its flavor.

OCTOPUS SEVICHE

1 pound octopus meat, fresh
    or thawed frozen,
    dressed, skinned, and
    tenderized
1 tablespoon ground dried
    chiles, or a few dashes of
    Tabasco

2 onions, thinly sliced
1 garlic clove, minced
1 teaspoon salt
1 tablespoon cracked
    peppercorns
1 cup lime juice
1 cup lemon juice

Wash the octopus. Remove the tentacles and slice into rings. Cut the body into 1-inch squares.

Put the octopus pieces and all the other ingredients in a glass, enamel or stainless-steel dish; mix well. Cover the dish and refrigerate, stirring from time to time, for 3 to 4 hours, or until octopus is white and opaque.

Drain. Serve on toothpicks at cocktail time.

4 to 6 servings

This recipe may be used also for squids.

OCTOPUS SOUP

1 pound octopus meat, fresh,
    thawed frozen or canned,
    dressed and skinned
1 cup Fish Stock (see Index)
    or clam broth
2 cups water
1 teaspoon salt

½ teaspoon dried thyme
few peppercorns
¼ pound salt pork, cubed
1 onion, chopped
½ green pepper, chopped
2 medium-size tomatoes,
    chopped
minced parsley

Pound the octopus meat until soft. Cut body into 1-inch squares and tentacles into rings.

Place octopus in a heavy pot with the stock, water and seasonings. Cover and simmer for 1 hour.

Remove the octopus pieces, put through a meat grinder, and return to the pot.

Sauté the salt pork in a heavy skillet. Add the onion and green pepper, and cook until onion is brown. Add the tomatoes and continue cooking for 5 minutes.

Add vegetable mixture to the soup pot. Simmer for a minute or so, check for seasoning, and serve garnished with parsley.

4 servings

OCTOPUS STEW IN WINE

1 fresh or thawed frozen
  octopus, 2 pounds,
  dressed and skinned
2 medium-size onions, finely
  chopped
2 garlic cloves, minced
2 tablespoons finely chopped
  parsley

½ teaspoon dried orégano
2 bay leaves
pinch of dried thyme
1 teaspoon salt
¼ cup olive oil
1 cup dry red wine
juice of ½ lemon

Pound the octopus meat until soft. Cut into 2-inch squares; slice the tentacles.

Sauté the onions, garlic, parsley, orégano, bay leaves, thyme and salt in hot oil until onions are brown.

Add the octopus pieces, and pour in the wine. Cover and simmer gently for 1½ hours, or until octopus is tender.

Remove the bay leaves and stir in the lemon juice.

4 servings

OCTOPUS IN "INK"

1 fresh or thawed frozen
  octopus, 2 pounds,
  dressed and skinned,
  "ink" reserved
2 onions, chopped
1 garlic clove, chopped

½ cup olive oil
1 teaspoon salt
dash of Tabasco
½ cup octopus "ink"
½ cup water

Pound the octopus meat until soft. Cut into 2-inch squares; slice the tentacles.

Sauté the onions and garlic in hot oil until onions are brown.

Add the octopus pieces, seasonings, "ink" and water. Cover and simmer for 2 hours, or until octopus is tender.

4 servings

FRIED OCTOPUS

2 pounds fresh octopus,
    dressed and skinned
1 teaspoon salt
½ teaspoon pepper

flour
4 tablespoons olive oil
minced parsley

Pound the octopus meat until soft. Cut into 2-inch squares; slice the tentacles.

Sprinkle with salt and pepper, and dust lightly with flour. Fry in hot oil for 1½ minutes on each side; do not overcook.

Serve garnished with parsley.

4 servings

This recipe may be used also for squids.

OCTOPUS CROQUETTES

1 cup flour
1 teaspoon baking powder
½ teaspoon salt
few grains of cayenne
1 cup milk
1 egg, beaten

2 cups finely chopped or
    ground cooked octopus
    meat
fat for frying
1 cup Béchamel Sauce (see
    Index)

Sift the dry ingredients together. Stir the milk and egg together. Beat the milk-egg mixture into the flour mixture, using a wire whisk, until batter is smooth.

Stir in the octopus meat. Drop batter by tablespoons into hot fat. Brown croquettes on both sides. Serve with béchamel sauce.

4 servings

This recipe may be used also for squids.

SQUIDS

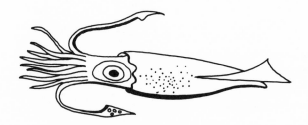

Contrary to popular belief, the Squid is not a variety of octopus. The two belong to totally different orders of cephalopod. The squid has a long, tubular cigar-shaped body; the octopus's body is globular. The squid has 10 suction-cupped tentacles; the octopus has 8. Both carry an ink sac which they use to becloud the water when predators attack. And they both swim at great speed by jet propulsion. They often differ greatly in size.

The average fishmarket squid runs 5 to 8 inches in body length, but deep-sea denizens have been discovered up to 6 feet. Most species of squid run in schools in moderately deep waters, rising to the surface at night to feed. They inhabit nearly all the oceans of the world.

Most native squids are taken commercially from the Monterey Bay in California, although the Mid-Atlantic Coast also yields a sizeable proportion.

The meat of the squid is sweet and tender, becoming tough only when carelessly overcooked. Like octopus lovers, squid lovers hail largely from the Oriental and Mediterranean countries. Almost all of the animal is eaten after the viscera have been cleaned away, making the squid one of the most efficient food machines of the sea.

How to Buy

In recent years squids have appeared increasingly in supermarkets and fish stores in most American big cities. This is because of improved freezing and packaging methods developed by the squid fishing industry. In considerable demand among people who have migrated here from Mediterranean countries, the little 6- to 8-inch squids are frozen and packaged, usually about a dozen to the box—total weight about 3 pounds. Fresh squids, sold by weight, are found in seafood stores and in some supermarkets.

In ports along the Adriatic a favorite seafood are baby squids or cuttlefish, called *calamaretti*. (A cuttlefish is another 10-armed cephalopod; unlike the squid, the cuttlefish still has a calcified internal shell. Nevertheless the names are used interchangeably and the cookery is similar.) True *calamaretti* are very tiny, with a taste between lobster and crab meat. You can find small squids, marketed as *calamaretti*, in seafood markets here, but they are not as tiny as the Adriatic species. If you cannot find any called that, just use the smallest squids available for the *calamaretti* recipes.

How to Prepare

If squids are frozen, defrost them. Wash with cold salted water. Cut off and reserve the tentacles. Cut off and discard the tail fins and about 1 inch of the tail. Cut off and discard the head, and pull out viscera and cartilage (the rudimentary shell).

Peel off the skin or membrane (a little hot water will help). The body may be left intact for stuffing, or can be sliced into rings or cut into fillets.

How to Store

Frozen squids may be kept in the freezer almost indefinitely. Once thawed, however, they may be refrozen only at the expense of flavor. Fresh squids are perishable and must be kept on ice. If the squid is not to be cooked within a reasonably short time, it should be frozen.

MARINATED CALAMARETTI

12 fresh calamaretti (baby squids), dressed and skinned
2 onions, thinly sliced
1 garlic clove, crushed

1 teaspoon salt
few peppercorns
few dashes of Tabasco
1 teaspoon paprika
2 cups lemon juice

Slice the bodies of the squids into strips. Place in a glass or enamel dish with all the other ingredients. Cover, and refrigerate for 3 hours, stirring from time to time.

Drain and serve with cocktails.

4 servings

STUFFED CALAMARETTI

12 fresh calamaretti (baby squids), dressed and skinned
1 garlic clove, minced
1 cup finely chopped fresh mushrooms

1 cup dry bread crumbs
½ teaspoon salt
½ teaspoon pepper
½ teaspoon dried orégano
1 tablespoon minced parsley
½ cup olive oil

Preheat oven to 375°F.

Wash the squids and dry thoroughly. Cut off and chop the tentacles. Mix the tentacles with the next 7 ingredients. Stuff the mixture into the body cavities of the *calamaretti*. Skewer.

Arrange squids in a baking dish, and brush with olive oil. Cover, and bake in the oven for about 45 minutes, basting occasionally.

4 servings

FRIED CALAMARETTI

12 fresh calamaretti (baby
   squids), dressed and
   skinned
flour
½ teaspoon salt
pepper

2 tablespoons butter
4 tablespoons olive oil
1 garlic clove, whole
minced parsley
4 lemon wedges

Wash the squids and dry thoroughly. Dust lightly with flour, salt and pepper to taste.

Heat the butter and oil in a heavy skillet. Add the garlic clove and sauté for 3 minutes. Remove and discard garlic.

Fry the *calamaretti* quickly, turning once, until brown and crisp.

Dust with parsley and serve with lemon wedges.

4 servings

SAUTÉED SQUIDS

8 fresh or thawed frozen
   squids, about 2 pounds,
   dressed and skinned
2 tablespoons butter
1 tablespoon olive oil
1 garlic clove, chopped
2 tablespoons chopped
   parsley

½ teaspoon salt
few grains of cayenne
¼ cup dry vermouth or white
   wine
4 lemon slices

Wash the squids, wipe them dry, and cut into serving-size pieces.

Heat the butter and oil in a heavy skillet and sauté the garlic, parsley and seasonings for 3 minutes.

Add the squid pieces and cook for 1½ minutes on each side.

Pour in the vermouth and simmer for 2 minutes longer. Serve with lemon slices.

4 servings

CURRIED SQUIDS

8 fresh or thawed frozen
  squids, about 2 pounds,
  dressed and skinned
2 tablespoons butter
2 tablespoons flour

1 teaspoon salt
1 tablespoon curry powder
1 cup Fish Stock (see Index)
4 slices of French bread,
  toasted

Wash the squids in salted cold water and slice into rings or serving-size squares.

Melt the butter in a heavy skillet; stir in the flour, salt and curry powder. Cook for 2 minutes, then stir in the stock and cook until sauce is smooth and thickened.

Add the squid pieces and simmer for about 3 minutes. Do not overcook.

Serve on toasted French bread.

4 servings

FRIED SQUIDS

8 fresh or thawed frozen
  squids, about 2 pounds,
  dressed and skinned
1 cup dry bread crumbs
1 teaspoon salt
1 teaspoon paprika
1 egg, beaten

2 cups oil
1 garlic clove
1 cup Sour-Cream
  Horseradish Sauce (see
  Index)
4 lemon slices

Wash the squids in salted cold water and wipe dry. Cut into rings or serving-size strips.

Mix together the crumbs, salt and paprika.

Dip the squid pieces into the beaten egg, then into the crumbs. Chill in the refrigerator for 30 minutes.

Heat the oil in a heavy skillet to the smoking point. Cook the garlic for 2 minutes and discard.

Quickly fry the squid pieces, a few at a time, until golden. Do not overcook.

Serve with sour-cream horseradish sauce and lemon slices.

4 servings

STUFFED SQUIDS

SQUIDS AND STUFFING

8 fresh or thawed frozen
    squids, about 2 pounds
2 garlic cloves, chopped
1 onion, chopped
2 tomatoes, chopped
3 tablespoons chopped
    parsley
3 tablespoons olive oil

3 egg yolks, lightly beaten
1 chunk of French bread, fist
    size, soaked in milk and
    squeezed dry
2 tablespoons water
dry bread crumbs
butter

SAUCE

1 onion, chopped
1 garlic clove, crushed
1 bay leaf
1 teaspoon salt

1 teaspoon pepper
2 tablespoons olive oil
½ cup flour
1 cup dry white wine

Preheat oven to 400°F.

Cut off the tentacles from the squids and chop into small pieces. Reserve. Cut off and discard the heads and tail fins of the squids. Draw the viscera and cartilage from the bodies and discard. Skin the bodies under warm water.

Mix the chopped tentacles with the garlic, onion, tomatoes and parsley. Sauté in the oil for 3 minutes, then stir in the egg yolks, soaked bread and water. Mix well and remove from the heat.

Stuff the body cavities of the squids almost full with this mixture, skewer, and arrange in a well-oiled sauté pan. Simmer gently, covered, for 30 minutes.

Prepare the sauce: Sauté the onion, garlic, bay leaf, salt and pepper in the oil for 3 minutes. Blend in the flour and stir in the wine. Simmer for 15 minutes. Remove the bay leaf. Pour sauce over the squids.

Sprinkle squids with bread crumbs, and dot with butter. Brown in the oven.

4 servings

Part Four

SHELLFISH
COMBINATIONS

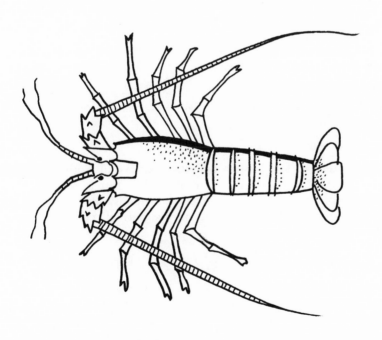

SHELLFISH ASOPAO A LA FAMILIA

3 slices of bacon, diced
½ cup diced ham
2 garlic cloves
1 medium-size onion,
    chopped
1 green bell pepper, chopped
1 red bell pepper, chopped
2 tomatoes, quartered
2 cups uncooked rice
6 cups hot water
1 teaspoon orégano
1 parsley sprig

3 tablespoons achiote fat (see
    Note)
1½ teaspoons salt
¼ teaspoon pepper
1 cup uncooked lobster meat
1 cup peeled uncooked
    shrimps
1 cup uncooked squid, sliced
    into rings, or uncooked
    cut-up conch
1 tablespoon capers

Sauté the bacon in a large pot. When half done, add the ham and cook for 2 minutes. Push aside; add the garlic, onion, peppers and tomatoes and cook for 5 minutes, stirring.

Add the rice; cook for 3 minutes, stirring. Add the water, herbs, achiote fat and seasonings; stir. Cover and simmer until the rice is cooked.

Add the shellfish and cook until the pieces are opaque, about 3 minutes. Sprinkle in the capers.

Serve in soup bowls. The *asopao* should not be as dry as *arroz con pollo* but should have the consistency of a thick soup. Serve as a main dish.

6 to 8 servings

Note: Achiote fat: Heat 3 tablespoons olive oil with ½ teaspoon *achiote annatto* in a small pan until all the color is extracted from the seeds. Discard the seeds. *Achiote annatto* is a Puerto Rican spice available at specialty shops and most supermarkets.

CURRIED SHRIMPS AND BEEF

4 tablespoons butter
2 tablespoons curry powder
2 cups uncooked rice
1 teaspoon salt
¼ teaspoon pepper
4½ cups Chicken Stock (see
    Index)
2 medium-size onions,
    chopped

2 celery ribs, diced, about 1
    cup
3 tablespoons peanut oil
1 pound uncooked shrimps,
    peeled and deveined
1 pound beef tenderloin, cut
    in ¾-inch cubes

Melt 2 tablespoons butter in a saucepan, add curry powder, and cook/stir for 2 minutes. Add the rice, salt, pepper and stock. Bring to a boil and cook covered over low heat until stock is absorbed, about 20 minutes.

In a large frying pan melt remaining 2 tablespoons butter and sauté onions and celery until light brown. Remove to a hot dish and reserve.

Pour the peanut oil into the same frying pan and heat it. Cook shrimps, stirring, for 3 minutes, until pink. Remove to the hot dish with the onion and celery.

Add the meat cubes to the pan and shake over medium heat until brown, about 4 minutes. Add the cooked rice and vegetable and shrimp mixture, and toss all together.

Serve with condiments such as chutney, peanuts, crumbled bacon, chopped preserved gingerroot, chopped fresh gingerroot, chopped hard-cooked egg, etc.

6 to 8 servings

CRAB-STUFFED LOBSTER

4 live lobsters, 1½ pounds
    each
½ pound butter, melted
1 cup fine dry bread crumbs
1 teaspoon salt
½ teaspoon freshly ground
    pepper

¼ cup Madeira or sherry wine
¼ cup light cream
2 cups cooked fresh crab meat
1 lemon, quartered

Kill the lobsters by inserting a sharp knife between body shell and tail. Split lobsters from head to tail, but do not cut through the shells. Remove and discard black vein and sac behind head; remove and reserve coral and tomalley; crack claws.

Preheat oven to 400°F.

Blend half of the melted butter with the reserved tomalley and coral, bread crumbs, seasonings, wine, cream, and crab meat.

Stuff the lobster cavities with this crab mixture, spreading remainder evenly over the top. Brush with remaining butter.

Bake in the oven until crumbs are golden brown. Serve with lemon wedges.

4 servings

MARYLAND STEAK AND OYSTERS

2½ pounds steak
   (porterhouse, shell or
   Delmonico)
1 pint shucked oysters
3 tablespoons melted butter

3 tablespoons lemon juice
1 teaspoon salt
½ cup boiling water
minced parsley

Trim excess fat from steak and broil in a heavy skillet for 4 minutes on each side. Remove to a shallow baking pan.

Heat the oysters in their liquor for a few minutes to start the juices; drain; spread oysters over the steak.

Blend the butter, lemon juice, salt and boiling water, and pour over the steak and oysters.

Bake in a preheated 375°F. oven for 10 minutes. Serve garnished with parsley.

4 servings

OYSTER AND HAM GUMBO

2 tablespoons butter
2 tablespoons flour
½ pound lean ham, diced
1 large onion, finely chopped
1 parsley sprig, chopped
1 thyme sprig, chopped
1 bay leaf, chopped

8 cups hot water and oyster
   liquor combined
4 dozen oysters
1½ teaspoons salt
¼ teaspoon pepper
2 tablespoons filé powder
1 cup cooked rice, hot

Melt the butter in a large kettle and stir in the flour. Simmer for 2 minutes, or until brown. Take care not to let the roux burn.

Add the ham and onion; stir until the onion is brown. Add the herbs and sauté for 2 minutes. Add the hot water and oyster liquor and bring to a boil.

Add the oysters and seasoning, and cook for 3 minutes. Remove from heat and add the filé powder. Stir vigorously and serve immediately. (Both oysters and the filé should be added just before serving.) Serve in soup bowls with a spoonful of rice.

4 to 6 servings

SEAFOOD STEW DIEPPOISE

3 tablespoons butter
1 leek, white part only, cut
   into thin slices
1 onion, thinly sliced
2 cups white wine
2 tomatoes, peeled and cut
   into quarters
1 sprig of fresh thyme, or ½
   teaspoon dried
1 bay leaf, finely chopped
1½ teaspoons salt

¼ teaspoon pepper
3 shallots, chopped
3 parsley sprigs, chopped
1 pound mussels, scrubbed
   and debearded
1 pound cod or turbot fillets
½ pound scallops
6 large shrimps, peeled
¾ pound fillet of halibut
¾ pound fillet of sole
1 cup heavy cream

In a large sauté pan or frying pan melt half of the butter over low heat. Sauté the leek and onion until transparent. Add the wine, tomatoes, thyme, bay leaf, salt and pepper. Simmer for 10 minutes.

In another pan with a cover, melt remaining butter. Add the shallots, parsley and mussels. Cover and cook for 4 to 5 minutes, or until the shells open. Remove from heat, but keep mussels warm.

Add the cod to the simmering vegetable and wine sauce; cook for 4 minutes. Add the scallops, shrimps, halibut and sole and simmer for 5 minutes. Remove cod, halibut and sole to a hot serving dish or soup plates.

Strain the liquid from the mussels into the sauce in which the fish fillets were cooked. Reduce liquid to half by boiling rapidly. Remove from heat, cool slightly, and add the cream, stirring.

Distribute mussels, still in shells, over the fillets and ladle sauce, scallops and shrimps over all.

6 to 8 servings

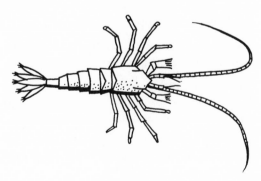

CLAM BELLIES AND SCALLOPS IN WINE

24 soft clams
4 tablespoons butter
4 tablespoons chopped
    shallots
½ cup dry white wine
1 cup bay scallops, or sea
    scallops cut into halves

1 teaspoon salt
½ teaspoon white pepper
½ cup cream
butter
1 tablespoon minced parsley

Scrub the clams. Place them in a heavy pot with 1 cup water and cook until shells open.

Cool. Remove clams from shells and remove the bellies, discarding or reserving the necks for another recipe. Cook the broth down to about ½ cup and reserve.

Melt 2 tablespoons of the butter and sauté the shallots for 1 minute, then stir in the wine. Simmer over low heat for 5 minutes.

Add the clam bellies, scallops, reserved broth, seasonings and cream. Cook for about 2 minutes. Garnish with bits of butter and parsley.

4 servings

This recipe may be used also for small oysters or mussels instead of the clam bellies.

PORTUGUESE CLAMS AND PORK CHOPS

4 pork chops, 1 inch thick
2 tablespoons olive oil
1 garlic clove, chopped
1 tablespoon chopped onion
1 tablespoon chopped parsley

1 cup liquid, half water, half
    wine, or half wine and
    half clam juice
1 pint small clams in shells

Sauté pork chops in the oil until brown on one side; turn and brown on the other side.

Add garlic and onion and cook until onion is light brown. Add parsley and cook for 2 minutes. Add liquid, cover, and simmer until chops are tender, 30 to 40 minutes.

Spread the clams, still in shells, over the pork chops. Cover pan with a tight-fitting lid and cook until the clams open, 3 to 5 minutes. Serve at once.

4 servings

CHICKEN AND OYSTERS

1 small chicken, about 3
    pounds, cut for frying
3 tablespoons butter
1 tablespoon chopped onion
2 tablespoons flour
12 shucked oysters with their
    liquor

½ cup Chicken Stock (see
    Index)
2 tablespoons heavy cream
2 tablespoons butter

Sauté chicken in hot butter over low heat without browning for 10 minutes. Turn and cook on the other side for 10 minutes.

Add the onion and cook until translucent. Sprinkle chicken pieces with flour and continue to cook, turning them in the butter and onion mixture.

In another pan simmer the oysters in their liquor for 3 minutes. Strain the oyster liquor into the stock and set the oysters aside. Add the stock and oyster liquor to the pan with the chicken and simmer for 10 minutes, or until chicken pieces are tender.

Add the cream and the butter in turn to the pan juices; mix. Add the oysters and heat briefly without boiling. Serve without delay.

4 servings

CLASSIC NEW ENGLAND CLAMBAKE

When summer comes and the New England weather becomes mild and enjoyable, people get together and cook up an old-fashioned clambake on one of the many beaches. Down through the years there have always been a chosen few well known for their skill as *bake masters,* and one of these is called in to take charge. Ingredients vary according to season and supply.

Here's how to do a clambake:

1. Dig a large hole in the sand and line it with rocks.
2. Build a fine, hot fire and lay on more large rocks.
3. When the rocks are good and hot, and the fire has died out, cover rocks with a layer of seaweed.
4. Add 6 live lobsters and another layer of seaweed.
5. Now, add 6 or 8 dozen scrubbed Cherrystone clams or

steamers, wrapped in cheesecloth, and a thick layer of seaweed.

6. Add a dozen ears of corn, unshucked but with silk removed, and 6 sweet potatoes in foil.
7. Cover with a canvas tarpaulin, weighted with rocks and banked with sand around the edges. Bake for 2 or 3 hours, or until clams begin to open.

Serve with plenty of beer.

6 servings

COMBINATION SHELLFISH FONDUE

Here's how to stage a shellfish fondue feast:

1. Prepare the shellfishes:
   Defrost and cube frozen rock lobster tails.
   Wash scallops, cut sea scallops into halves, leave bays whole.
   Shuck oysters.
   Shuck Little Neck clams.
   Shuck mussels.
   Peel and devein shrimps.
2. Prepare the sauces (see Index): Béarnaise Sauce, Curry Cream Sauce, Supreme Cocktail Sauce, Caper Sauce, Sauce Rémoulade, etc.
3. Cut lemons into wedges.
4. Prepare the fondue pot: Heat oil to a sizzle and keep hot over a low flame.
5. Pour chilled white wine or cold beer.
6. Feast yourself: Impale a morsel of shellfish on a 2-tined long-handled fondue fork; immerse shellfish in the hot oil and sizzle for a minute or so, or until shellfish becomes opaque. Dip shellfish into one or more of the sauces. Quench with wine or beer.

PAELLA VALENCIANA

3 tablespoons olive oil
2 garlic cloves, finely chopped
2 medium-size onions,
    chopped
2 red bell peppers, seeded
    and chopped
1 small chicken, 2½ pounds,
    cut for frying, or chicken
    parts
3 ounces ham, diced
4 tomatoes, peeled, seeded
    and quartered
2 cups uncooked rice, washed
4 cups Chicken Stock (see
    Index)

1 teaspoon whole saffron,
    soaked in ¼ cup hot
    water
1 cup shelled peas
1 lobster in shell, cut into
    pieces
½ pound uncooked shrimps,
    shelled and deveined
2 cups small clams in shells,
    scrubbed
2 pounds squids, dressed,
    skinned and sliced
    (optional)

Heat the oil in a paella pan or large frying pan with a lid. Sauté garlic, onions and peppers until onions are translucent.

Push vegetables aside and add the chicken pieces. Sauté chicken until lightly browned on both sides. Add the ham and cook for a few minutes.

Add tomatoes and rice. Cook, stirring gently, for 5 minutes. Add the stock, saffron liquid and peas. Cover the pan and cook over medium heat for 10 minutes.

Add the lobster pieces and shrimps and cook over high heat for 5 minutes, then simmer for 15 minutes.

Add the clams and squids on top, cover, and cook for 4 minutes.

8 to 10 servings

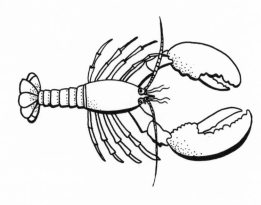

LOUISIANA SHELLFISH GUMBO

1 teaspoon ground allspice
1 teaspoon chopped celery
    leaves
1 bay leaf
1 teaspoon salt
⅛ teaspoon dried thyme
½ teaspoon pepper
1 hot red pepper pod
4 cups boiling water
12 shucked oysters

2 cups shelled raw shrimps
2-inch cube of salt pork, diced
1 large onion, chopped
1 green pepper, chopped
1 garlic clove, chopped
1 celery rib, chopped
2 tablespoons flour
2 cups chopped tomatoes
2 cups chopped okra, fresh or
    thawed frozen

Put the spices and seasonings into a large pot with the boiling water and cook for 5 minutes. (This is a court bouillon.)

Add the shellfishes and poach them for 5 minutes. Strain, reserving the shellfishes and the broth.

Sauté the salt pork in a large pot until crisp; remove and reserve cracklings.

Sauté all the vegetables except tomatoes and okra in the pork fat for 5 minutes; stir in the flour and cook for 5 minutes longer.

Add the tomatoes and okra and the reserved broth. Cover and simmer for 1 hour.

Add the reserved shellfishes and pork cracklings. Heat and serve.

4 to 6 servings

SHELLFISHES EN BROCHETTE

8 large shrimps, peeled and
    deveined
8 large mussels
8 sea scallops, washed and
    dried
8 fresh mushroom caps,
    washed and dried

flour
2 eggs, beaten with ½
    teaspoon salt and ¼
    teaspoon pepper
fresh bread crumbs
4 teaspoons Dijon mustard
¼ pound butter

Poach the shrimps in salted water for 5 minutes; drain.

Steam the mussels in ¼ cup water until shells open; remove mussels, discard the shells.

Arrange the shrimps, mussels, scallops and mushrooms alternately on four 8-inch skewers, two of each kind of shellfish per skewer.

Roll the skewers in flour and coat with seasoned egg. Roll in bread crumbs and dab each skewer with 1 teaspoon mustard.

Heat the butter in a heavy skillet and sauté the skewers for about 4 minutes on each side, or until golden brown.

4 servings

FLORIDA SEAFOOD STEW

½ cup oil
1 large onion, chopped
2 leeks, white parts only,
    chopped
2 garlic cloves, chopped
2 tomatoes, peeled and
    chopped
1 bay leaf

2 teaspoons salt
2 teaspoons peppercorns
1½ pounds pompano fillets,
    cut up
2 cups cut-up rock lobster tails
1 dozen softshell clams,
    scrubbed
½ cup dry white wine

Heat the oil and sauté the onion, leeks and garlic until golden.

Stir in the tomatoes, bay leaf, salt and peppercorns.

Add the pompano, lobster, clams and enough boiling water to cover.

Lower the heat, cover, and cook for 7 minutes, or until pompano flakes easily and clam shells open.

Discard the bay leaf, stir in the wine, and heat through. Serve in bowls.

4 to 6 servings

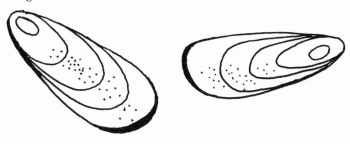

BOUILLABAISSE MARSEILLAISE

½ cup olive oil
1 carrot, chopped
2 medium-size onions,
  chopped
1 leek, white part only,
  chopped
2 cups chopped tomatoes
1 large garlic clove, minced
1 bay leaf
few threads of saffron
few grains of cayenne
1 teaspoon salt
1 pound eel, eviscerated and
  skinned

1 pound each of 2 firm fishes
  (cod, mullet, haddock,
  whiting, sea bass), dressed
2 cups cooked lobster meat,
  cut up, or cooked
  shrimps
16 mussels or Little Neck
  clams, scrubbed
1½ cups water
¼ pound butter
½ cup flour
1 cup dry white wine
crusty French garlic bread

Heat the oil in a large deep skillet or pot and put in the vegetables and seasonings. Cover and cook briskly for 5 minutes.

Add the eel, the 2 fishes, the shellfish, mollusks and water. Cover and simmer slowly until mollusks open.

Remove the fishes, cut off and discard the heads, tails, fins and skin. Cut fishes into 4 equal pieces, place in a napkin, and keep warm.

Melt the butter in a small saucepan; stir in the flour. Strain the broth and stir it into the roux; cook, stirring, until sauce is thickened and smooth; stir in the wine.

Pour sauce into 4 large bowls and serve with the napkins of fish. (Fish pieces are dipped into the sauce and eaten with the crusty bread.)

4 servings

FISHERMAN'S WHARF CIOPPINO

2 uncooked Dungeness crabs
1 pound uncooked shrimps in the shell
1 pound firm fish (sea bass, cod, halibut, etc.), dressed and cut into 2-inch pieces
2 cups chopped onions
1 garlic clove, chopped
1 cup chopped parsley
1 cup olive oil
1 teaspoon salt
½ teaspoon pepper
2 cups chopped tomatoes
1 cup tomato sauce
¼ cup chopped fresh basil
1 dozen Little Neck clams, scrubbed

Split the crabs, clean them, crack the claws, but leave the meat in the shells.

Put all the ingredients except basil and clams into a heavy pot, cover, and simmer for 20 minutes.

Add the basil and clams and cook, uncovered, for 20 minutes longer. Serve in bowls.

6 servings

Part Five

STOCKS, SAUCES AND STUFFINGS

FISH STOCK

2 pounds fish trimmings
  (heads, bones, tails)
1 onion, thinly sliced
6 parsley sprigs
1 teaspoon lemon juice

1 cup dry white wine
  (optional)
2 quarts cold water
½ teaspoon peppercorns

Put all the ingredients into a soup kettle and bring to a boil. Reduce heat and simmer for about 1 hour.

Strain. If not for immediate use, refrigerate. Or freeze in airtight containers if not to be used within 2 days.

2 quarts

FISH FUMET

A *fumet* is a concentrate made by reducing wine-based fish stock. It gives shellfish cooking extra richness.

Put 2 quarts fish stock made with wine (or add 1 quart wine to plain stock) in an uncovered kettle and simmer until reduced to half the quantity. If not for immediate use, cool, place in airtight containers, and refrigerate. Or freeze if not to be used within 2 days.

SHELLFISH STOCK

shellfish shells and scraps
2 cups water
1 onion, chopped
6 parsley sprigs

dash of Tabasco
1 cup dry wine, red or white
  (optional)
2 cups clam broth

Put the shells and scraps into a pot, pour in the water, and simmer, covered, for about 30 minutes. Strain the broth; discard the scraps.

Add remaining ingredients to the broth, bring to a boil, then reduce the heat and simmer for about 1 hour.

Cool. Strain into an airtight container and refrigerate; or freeze, if stock is not to be used within 2 days.

about 3 cups

CHICKEN STOCK

1 small chicken, 2½ pounds,
    or giblets, bones and
    trimmings
1 veal knuckle
1 onion stuck with a clove

1 carrot, peeled
1 teaspoon salt
⅛ teaspoon pepper
5 cups water, or to cover

Put everything in a stockpot and bring to a boil. Skim carefully during first 5 minutes. Simmer gently for 1½ to 2 hours.

Cool, skim, remove chicken or parts and veal knuckle. Strain stock. Refrigerate if not for immediate use.

about 3½ cups

VELOUTÉ SAUCE

1 tablespoon butter
2 tablespoons flour
1 cup Chicken Stock
    (preceding recipe)

1 tablespoon heavy cream
¼ teaspoon salt
⅛ teaspoon pepper

Melt the butter in a small frying pan over low heat. Stir in the flour and sauté for 2 minutes.

Gradually stir in the stock until sauce thickens to the desired consistency. Remove from heat and add the cream, salt and pepper.

about 1 cup

FISH VELOUTÉ

4 tablespoons butter
4 tablespoons flour
2 cups Fish Fumet
    (preceding page)

1 cup cream
½ teaspoon salt
pinch of white pepper

Melt the butter in a heavy saucepan and stir in the flour. Cook for 1 minute.

Stir in the *fumet* and simmer for 15 minutes.

Stir in the cream and seasonings. Simmer the sauce, under the boiling point, until smooth and thickened.

2 cups

WHITE-WINE COURT BOUILLON
(FOR POACHING)

1 quart water
1 quart dry white wine
2 onions, thinly sliced
1 bay leaf

few parsley sprigs
½ teaspoon peppercorns
½ teaspoon salt

Put all the ingredients into a soup kettle, cover, and simmer for 30 minutes.

Strain. If not for immediate use, refrigerate. Or freeze, if not to be used within 2 days. Bring to room temperature before using it. Court bouillon can be strained after using and reused.

1 ½ quarts

BÉCHAMEL SAUCE (BASIC WHITE SAUCE)

4 tablespoons butter
4 tablespoons flour
2 teaspoons grated onion
½ teaspoon salt

pinch of white pepper
pinch of grated nutmeg
2 cups milk or half-and-half

Melt the butter in a heavy saucepan. Stir in the flour, onion and seasonings. Do not brown.

Slowly stir in the milk and cook until sauce is smooth and creamy.

about 2 cups

CURRY CREAM SAUCE

Make 2 cups Béchamel sauce, stirring 2 teaspoons curry powder into the melted butter before cooking.

EGG SAUCE

Make 2 cups Béchamel sauce; stir in 3 finely chopped hard-cooked eggs.

HERB SAUCE

Make 2 cups Béchamel sauce, stirring 1½ tablespoons chopped fresh herbs (parsley, chives, dill), or 1 tablespoon dried, into the butter before cooking.

MUSHROOM SAUCE

Make 2 cups Béchamel sauce, stirring ½ cup finely chopped mushrooms into the melted butter before cooking.

MORNAY SAUCE

Make 2 cups Béchamel sauce. Lightly beat 1 egg yolk, stir in a little of the sauce to warm the egg, then pour egg mixture into remaining sauce and bring to a boil. Stir in ½ cup grated Gruyère or Parmesan cheese, or a combination of both.

HOLLANDAISE SAUCE

3 egg yolks
2 tablespoons lemon juice or
    vinegar
pinch of salt

few grains of cayenne
¼ pound butter (1 stick),
    clarified
3 tablespoons hot water

In the top section of a double boiler, over hot water, beat the egg yolks, 1 tablespoon lemon juice, salt and cayenne with a wire whisk until smooth.

Heat the butter and add teaspoon by teaspoon.

Add water and continue whisking as sauce thickens.

Add the remaining lemon juice. Remove from heat, but keep warm over lukewarm water. This sauce is served warm, rather than hot.

about 1 cup

BLENDER HOLLANDAISE

Put egg yolks, lemon juice, salt and cayenne into a blender container. Do not start blender until the butter is melted. (In the blender method, the eggs are cooked only by the hot butter, so it must be very hot.)

Melt butter in a small saucepan. When butter is *very hot* start blender on medium speed. As soon as it reaches full speed, uncover the container and pour in hot butter in a steady stream. At the last second add the hot water, to stabilize the emulsion. As soon as the mixture thickens, in 5 to 10 seconds, turn off the blender. Keep sauce warm over hot water.

about 1 cup

BÉARNAISE SAUCE

2 shallots, chopped
2 sprigs of fresh tarragon,
    chopped, or 1 teaspoon
    dried
2 sprigs of fresh chervil,
    chopped, or 1 teaspoon
    dried
¼ bay leaf, chopped

¼ teaspoon salt
pinch of white pepper
¼ cup white wine
¼ cup tarragon vinegar
3 egg yolks
1 tablespoon water
¼ pound (1 stick) butter,
    clarified

Put shallots, herbs, seasonings, wine and vinegar in a small pan and cook until reduced to one third of the original quantity. Cool.

Add the egg yolks and water and beat with a whisk over hot water just under boiling. When the yolks begin to thicken, add the butter, teaspoon by teaspoon, whisking each teaspoon in before adding another until all the butter is used. (This can be done over direct low heat if the pan is held over it just to keep the mixture hot but removed from the heat while whisking. Great care must be taken to prevent overheating.)

Keep finished sauce warm over hot water until ready to use.

about 1½ cups

BLENDER BÉARNAISE

Use the same method as for Blender Hollandaise. Cook shallots and herb mixture first and cool it. Scrape herb mixture into a blender container and add egg yolks. With blender at full speed, add the hot butter. Finally add the water.

Note: To clarify butter, melt it over low heat, then pour the liquid fat into a separate pan, leaving white sediment in first pan.

MAYONNAISE

3 egg yolks, chilled (see Note)
½ teaspoon salt
pinch of white pepper
1½ tablespoons lemon juice,
    chilled

1 cup vegetable oil mixed with
    1 cup olive oil, chilled
boiling water

Put egg yolks into a chilled bowl. Add seasonings and a few drops of the lemon juice. Mix lightly with a wire whisk.

While whisking, add the oil, drop by drop at first, then in a thin trickle. Continue this action, thinning down occasionally with a few more drops of lemon juice.

When the sauce is finished, whisk in 1 to 2 tablespoons boiling water to prevent curdling. (Mayonnaise made entirely with olive oil is more likely to separate. If separation takes place, put an egg yolk into a bowl and gradually beat the mayonnaise into it.)

3 cups

Note: For stable emulsion and the successful making of mayonnaise, it is essential that *all* ingredients and utensils be chilled to the same temperature, or all warmed to room temperature.

SAVORY MAYONNAISE

Follow the recipe for mayonnaise. Before adding oil, whisk in 2 teaspoons anchovy paste; or *fines herbes* (chopped chives, parsley, chervil, tarragon); or ¼ teaspoon curry powder and 2 teaspoons snipped chives; or 2 teaspoons dry mustard; or 1 tablespoon tomato purée.

TARTAR SAUCE

Blend together ¾ cup mayonnaise, 1 teaspoon finely chopped shallot or onion, 1 teaspoon finely chopped sweet pickle, 1 teaspoon finely chopped stuffed olive.

SAUCE VINAIGRETTE

1 hard-cooked egg yolk
½ teaspoon Dijon mustard
1 tablespoon vinegar
1 teaspoon finely chopped
    onion
1 teaspoon finely chopped
    capers

½ teaspoon salt
few grains of cayenne
4 tablespoons olive oil
1 tablespoon lemon juice

Mash the cooked egg yolk until smooth. Add mustard, vinegar, onion, capers and seasonings; blend thoroughly.

Add the oil, continuing to mix, and lastly add the lemon juice.

about ½ cup

SAUCE RAVIGOTE

4 shallots, minced
2 tablespoons butter
½ teaspoon dry mustard
1 cup dry white wine

½ teaspoon sugar
2 tablespoons tomato paste
½ teaspoon salt

Sauté the shallots in the butter for about 10 minutes, or until golden.

Add remaining ingredients and simmer for 20 minutes.

about 1 ¼ cups

SAUCE RÉMOULADE

1 teaspoon dry mustard
1 anchovy, finely chopped
1 gherkin, finely chopped
3 hard-cooked egg yolks,
    chopped
4 tablespoons light olive oil
2 tablespoons vinegar
1 teaspoon salt
⅛ teaspoon pepper

1½ teaspoons capers, finely
    chopped

or 1 cup mayonnaise

HOME-STYLE RÉMOULADE Put all ingredients in a food processor; or push first 4 ingredients through a sieve with egg yolks, oil and vinegar, salt and pepper.

about ½ cup

RESTAURANT-STYLE RÉMOULADE Mix first 4 ingredients with 1 cup mayonnaise and put through a sieve.

about 1 cup

CAPER SAUCE (FOR HOT SHELLFISH)

¼ pound butter
6 tablespoons capers

1 tablespoon lemon juice

Melt the butter, add the capers and lemon juice, and simmer for 2 minutes.

¾ cup

CAPER SAUCE WITH ANCHOVIES
(FOR CHILLED SHELLFISH)

½ cup olive oil
3 anchovies, finely chopped

6 tablespoons capers

Mix all the ingredients together and let stand for 30 minutes.

¾ cup

SOUR-CREAM HORSERADISH SAUCE

1 cup dairy sour cream
1 tablespoon prepared
    horseradish

1 tablespoon minced parsley

Mix all the ingredients together and chill in the refrigerator.

1 cup

MIGNONETTE SAUCE (FOR OYSTERS)

¼ cup chopped shallots
½ cup red-wine vinegar
½ teaspoon cracked whole
    peppercorns

pinch of salt

Mix all the ingredients together and chill in the refrigerator.

¾ cup

SAUCE NANTUA

2 tablespoons butter
3 tablespoons flour
½ teaspoon salt
⅛ teaspoon white pepper
1 cup hot milk

¼ cup cream
1 teaspoon onion juice
3 tablespoons crayfish butter,
    or ½ cup liquid in which
    crayfish were cooked

Melt the butter in a saucepan and stir in the flour. Add salt, pepper and milk slowly until sauce is smooth and thickened.

Stir in the cream and onion juice (and crayfish liquid, if used) and cook over low heat until sauce is reduced to one third.

Stir the crayfish butter (if used) into the sauce and cook for 1 minute. Put into an airtight container and refrigerate, or freeze if not to be used immediately.

about 2 cups

CRAYFISH BUTTER

Sauté the shells of about 3 dozen crayfishes in ½ pound unsalted butter for 5 or 6 minutes. Let steep over very low heat for about 10 minutes longer.

Mix in a food processor fitted with the steel blade until smooth. Put through a sieve or food mill. Chill until firm. Cut into pieces to use as a dressing, or measure out in tablespoons to add to sauces.

This recipe may be used also for lobster or crab shells.

BEURRE NOIR

Melt ¼ pound butter in a small pan and cook until brown, not black. Add 1 teaspoon lemon juice and season to taste. Use at once. (This butter can be prepared in the pan used for frying fish.)

½ cup

BEURRE BLANC

Melt ¼ pound butter in a small pan. Stir in ¼ cup finely snipped chives and cook, stirring, for 1 minute. Add ¼ cup white-wine vinegar and cook down to half. Add ½ cup dry white wine and cook until wine has nearly evaporated. Use at once.

½ cup

MAÎTRE D'HÔTEL BUTTER

¼ pound butter, softened   ⅛ teaspoon pepper
1 tablespoon chopped parsley   1 teaspoon lemon juice
1 teaspoon salt

Mix all ingredients together to form a paste. Use cold or warm to dress shellfish, or use melted to cook shellfish.

MEUNIÈRE BUTTER

4 tablespoons butter   1 teaspoon lemon juice

Melt butter until it turns light brown. Add lemon juice. Pour over shellfish just before serving.

Shellfish can also be cooked in the butter as it colors.

LEMON BUTTER

¼ pound butter, softened   grated rind of 1 lemon

Mix well; use to season shellfish.

DRAWN BUTTER

In the top section of a double boiler, over hot water, blend together 2 tablespoons melted butter, 2 tablespoons flour, ½ teaspoon salt and a little pepper. Stir in 1 cup hot fish stock or 1 cup hot water, and bring to a boil. Add 1 teaspoon lemon juice and 2 additional tablespoons unmelted butter, cut into little pieces. The sauce is ready when the butter is melted.

1¼ cups

CRAB BOIL

Crab Boil (also called Shrimp Spice) is a seasoning mixture sold in seafood stores and in many supermarkets. Use during the steaming of crabs, shrimps, crayfishes, lobsters, etc., and for seasoning crab cakes, imperial crab and many shellfish soups; it is a handy seasoning to have around.

It can be safely stated that there are no two commercial crab boils alike. To make your own, mix together almost any of the seasonings you might have on hand. Or sift together the following ingredients: 1 cup salt, ½ cup paprika, 1 teaspoon each of pepper, dry mustard, cloves, bay leaves, mace, cardamom, ginger, cassia. All of the spices must, of course, be finely ground.

SUPREME COCKTAIL SAUCE

1 cup ketchup
1 tablespoon tarragon vinegar
1 tablespoon prepared horse-
    radish
1 tablespoon minced onion

½ teaspoon salt
1 tablespoon Worcestershire
    sauce
2 drops of Tabasco

Mix all the ingredients together and chill.

1¼ cups

SHELLFISH STUFFING

4 tablespoons butter
1 onion, minced
1 teaspoon salt
pinch each of thyme, basil,
    paprika and pepper
2 cups fresh bread crumbs
1 egg, well beaten

1 cup cooked crab meat, or
    drained chopped raw
    clams, or minced cooked
    lobster, or drained
    chopped oysters, or
    minced cooked shrimps
fish stock or clam broth
    (optional)

Melt the butter and sauté the onion until golden. Add the season-ings.

Stir in bread crumbs, egg and shellfish, and mix well. Moisten if desired with fish stock or clam broth.

about 3 cups

BREAD-CRUMB STUFFING

2 tablespoons butter
2 tablespoons olive oil
2 tablespoons finely chopped
    onion
2 tablespoons minced parsley

1 teaspoon salt
¼ teaspoon pepper
2 cups fresh coarse bread
    crumbs

Heat the butter and oil, and sauté the onion until translucent.

Add remaining ingredients and toss until well mixed.

2 cups

GARLIC STUFFING

Add 1 garlic clove, finely chopped, to Bread-Crumb Stuffing, with the onion, and sauté until translucent.

HERB STUFFING

Add ½ teaspoon dried thyme (for mussels); 1 teaspoon dried dill (for shrimps or lobsters); or 1 teaspoon dried rosemary, or 1 teaspoon ground sage, or 1 teaspoon dried marjoram. Add herb to butter and oil while sautéing onion.

INDEX